# ANSWERS

# Essential Music Theory

## Levels 4-6

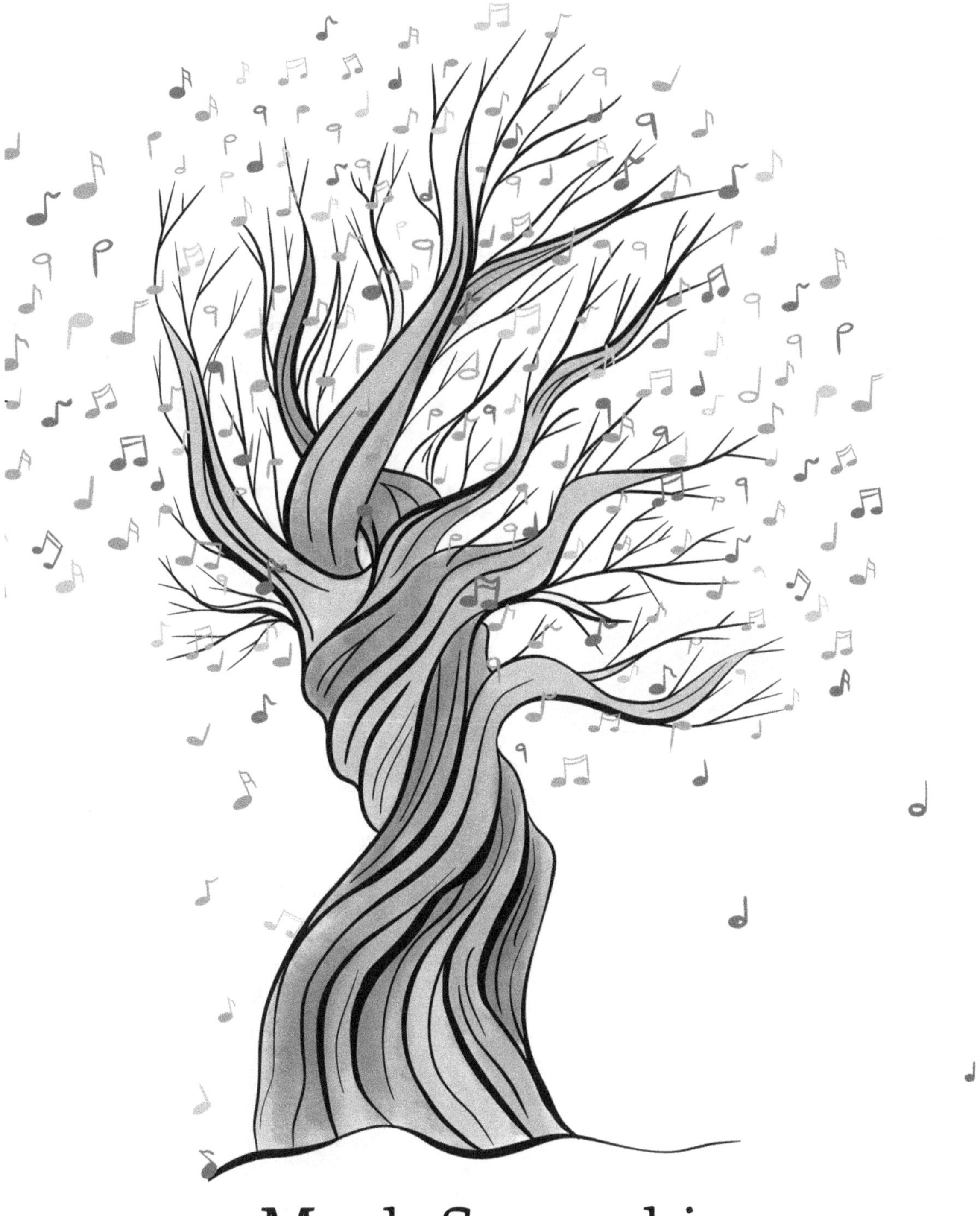

San Marco Publications

Mark Sarnecki

Elementary Music Theory © 2024 by San Marco Publications. All rights reserved.

All right reserved. No part of this book may be reproduced in any form or by electronic or mechanical means including Information storage and retrieval systems without permission in writing from the author.

ISNB: 9781896499505

# Level 4-6 Answers

Page 4, No. 1

Page 4, No. 2

Page 4, No. 3

Page 6, No. 1

Page 6, No. 2

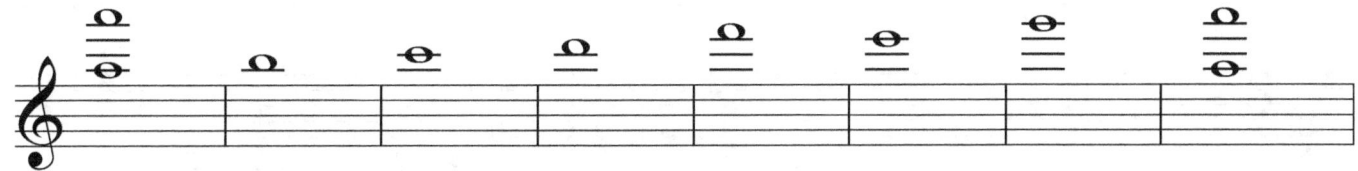

Page 6, No. 3

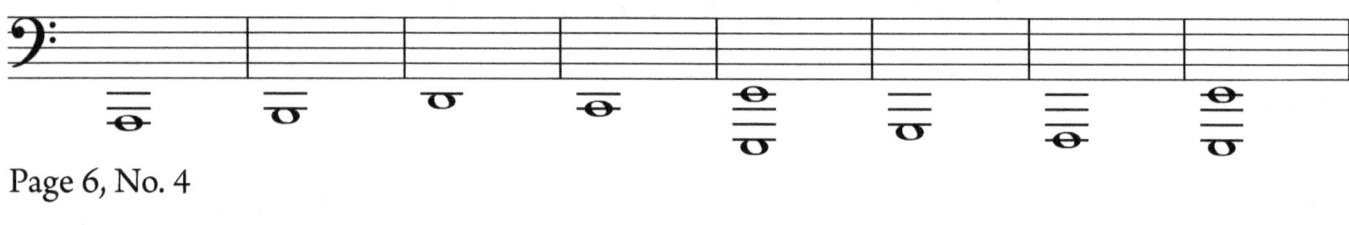

Page 6, No. 4

Page 7, No. 5

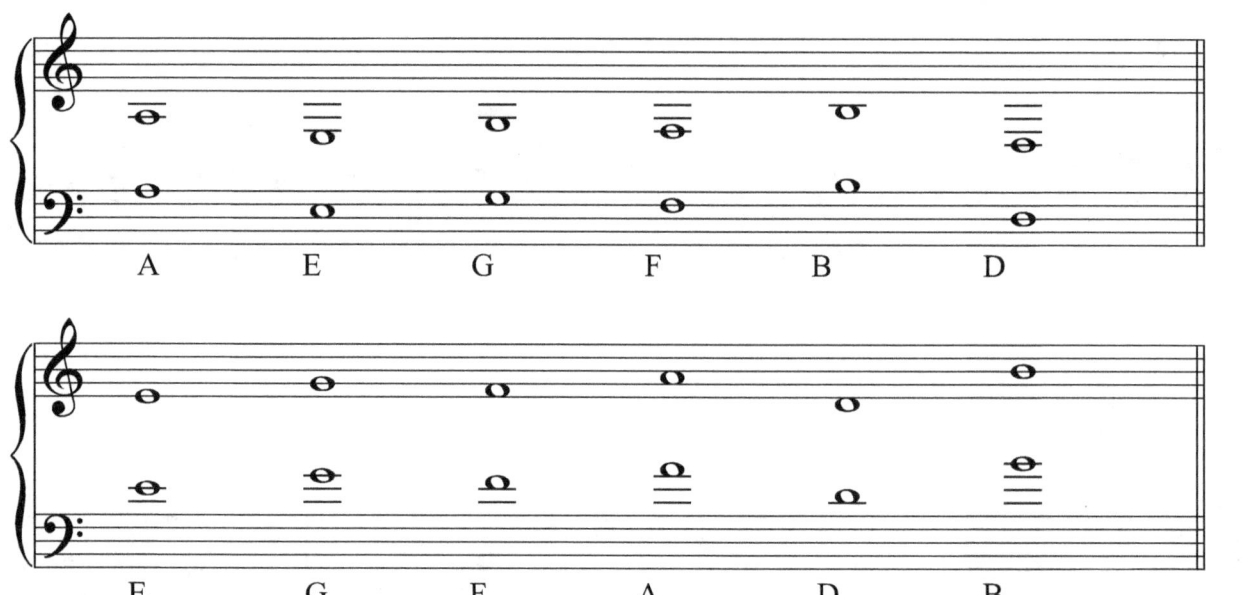

Page 7, No. 6

Jean Sibelius
Symphony No. 3, III

Page 8, No. 1

| G♭ | B♭ | E# |
| A# | C♭ | F# |
| D♭ | A♭ | C# |
| E♭ | B# | G# |
| F  | A# | D# |

Page 10, No. 1

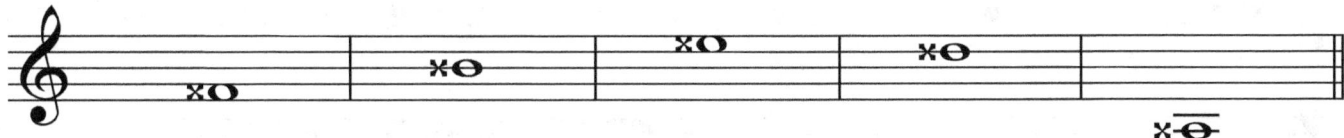

Page 10, No. 2

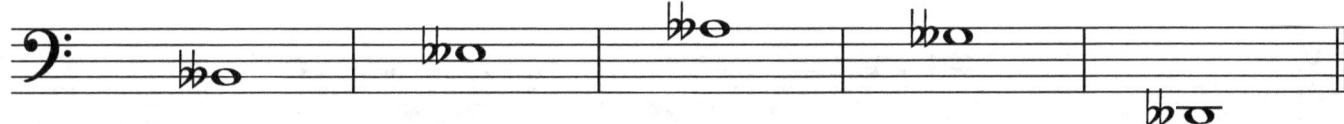

Page 11, No. 1

Page 12, No. 2

Jean Sibelius
Symphony No. 3, III

Wolfgang Amadeus Mozart
Piano Concerto K270

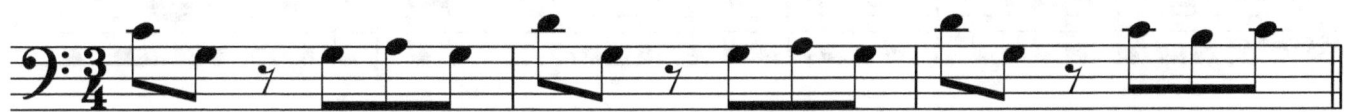

Page 14, No. 1

Page 14, No. 2

| 3/4 | 3/4 |
| --- | --- |
| 2/4 | 2/4 |
| 4/4 | 4/4 |
| 3/4 | 4/4 |
| 2/4 | 3/4 |

Page 16, No. 1

Page 16, No. 2

3/4

2/4

4/4

3/4

Page 18, No. 1

4/8 or 2/4

2/8

3/8

4/8 or 2/4

2/8

3/8

Page 19, No. 2

Page 20, No. 3

Page 23, No. 1

Page 23, No. 2

Page 24, No. 3

Page 26, No. 1

2/4   2/2   2/4   2/8   2/2   2/8   2/4

Page 28, No. 1

Ludwig van Beethoven
Symphony No. 9, IV

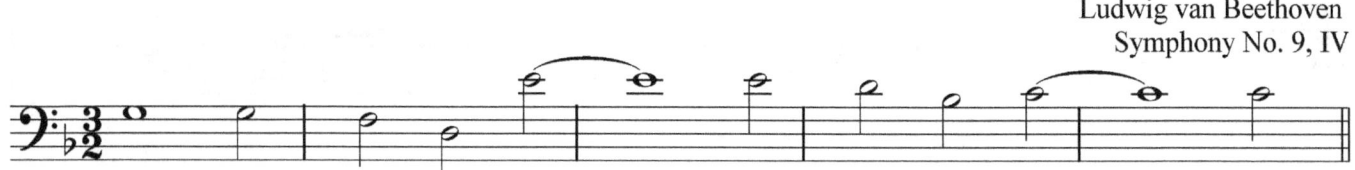

Page 30, No. 1

4/2   4/4   4/2   4/4

Page 31, No. 2

Page 31, No. 3

4/4   4/2   3/2

Page 32, No. 1

Page 32, No. 2

Page 33, No. 1

| 2/4 | 3/8 |
| 4/4 | 3/2 |
| 3/4 | 2/8 |

Page 34, No. 1

Page 35, No. 2

Page 37, No. 1

Page 38, No. 2

3/4
6/8
6/8
3/4

Page 38, No. 3

Page 39, No. 1

Page 40, No. 2

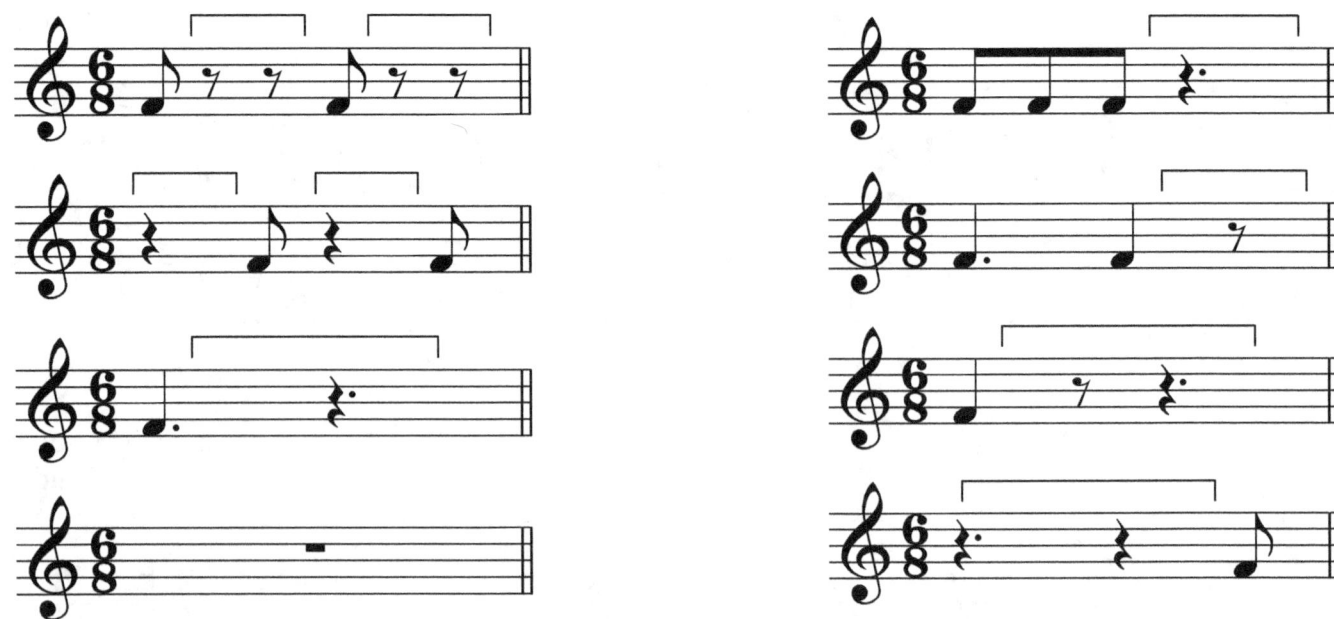

Page 42, No. 1

a. Sixteenth note.

b. Eighth note.

c. Half note.

d. Dotted quarter note.

e. Whole note.

f. Quarter note.

Page 42, No. 2

2/4
3/8
2/4
4/4
3/4

Page 43, No. 1

Page 44, No. 2

Page 46, No. 1

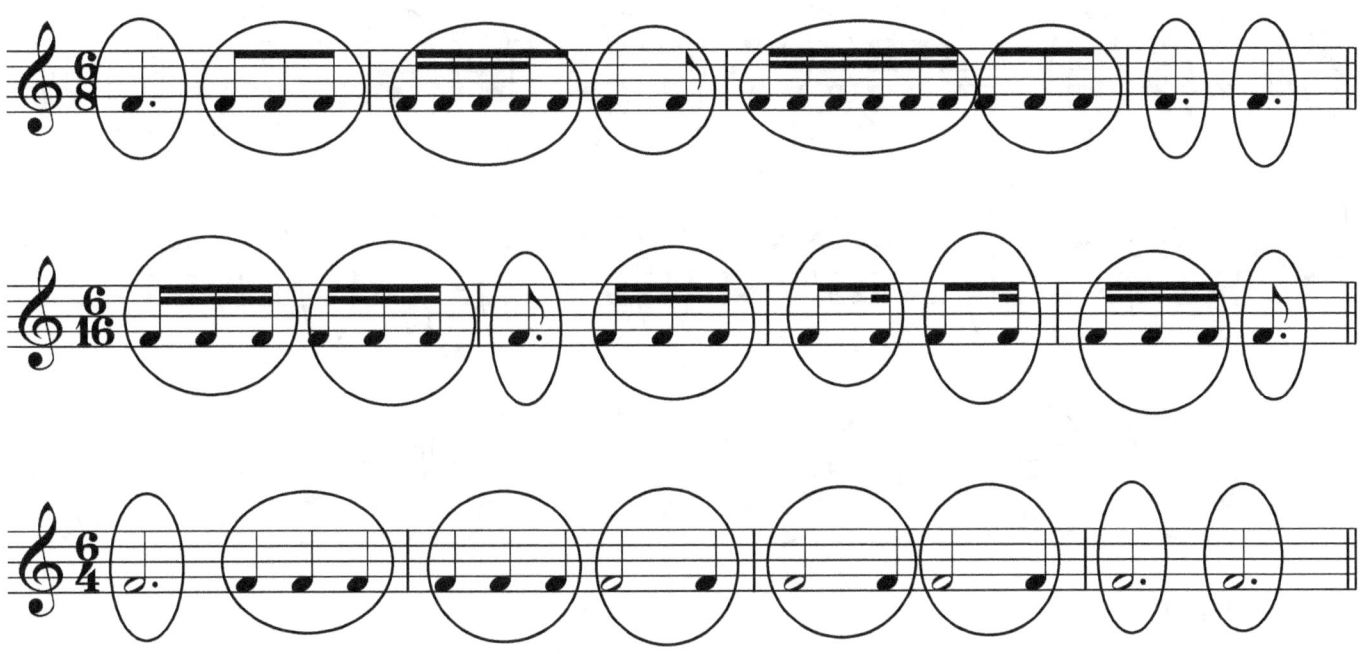

Page 47, No. 2

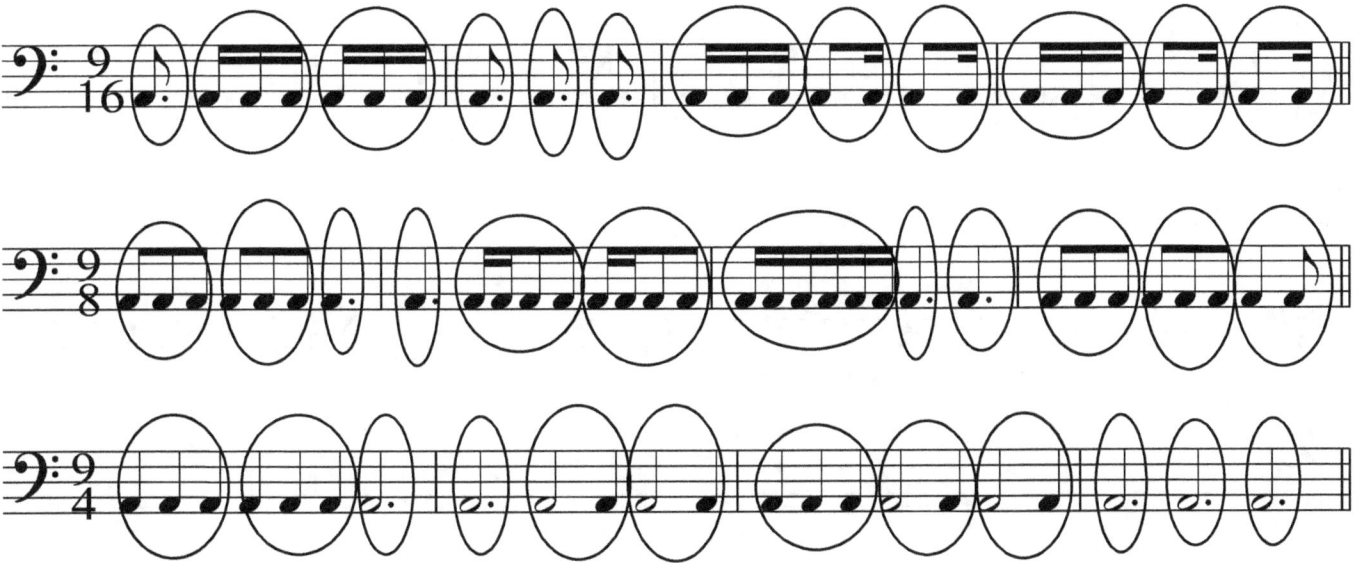

Page 48, No. 3

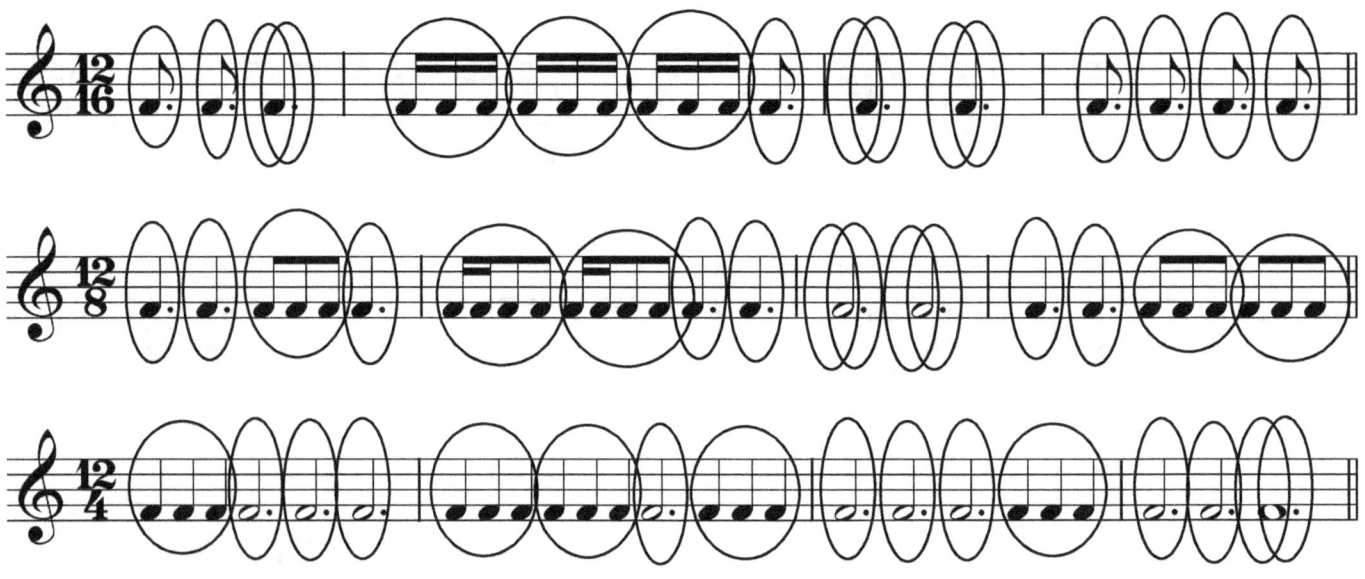

Page 49, No. 4

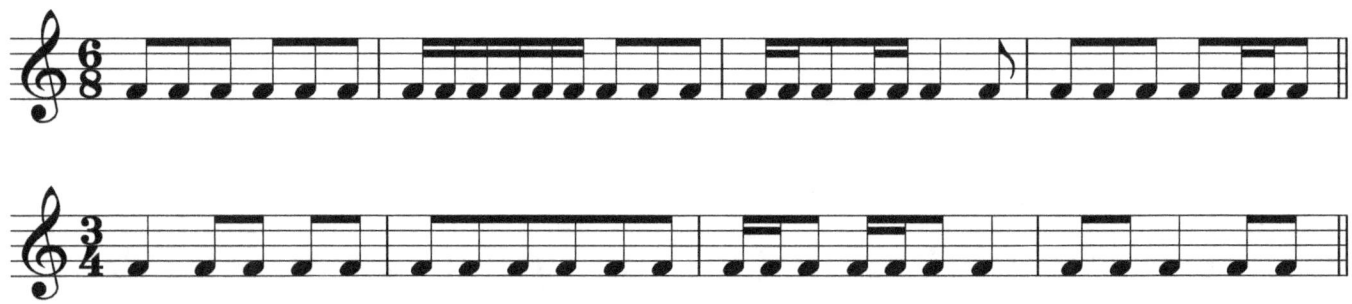

Page 51, No. 5

Page 52, No. 5

Page 52-53, No. 6

12/8
6/8
3/2
9/8
4/2
4/4
6/8
2/4
9/8
12/8

Page 56, No. 1

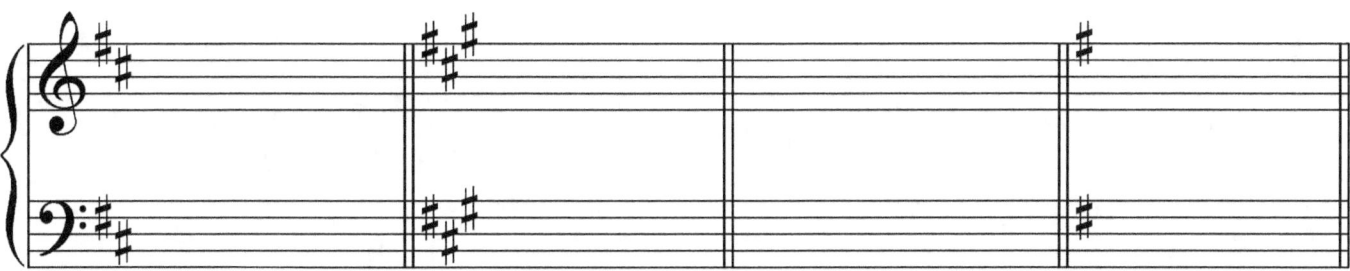

Page 56, No. 2

Page 58, No. 1

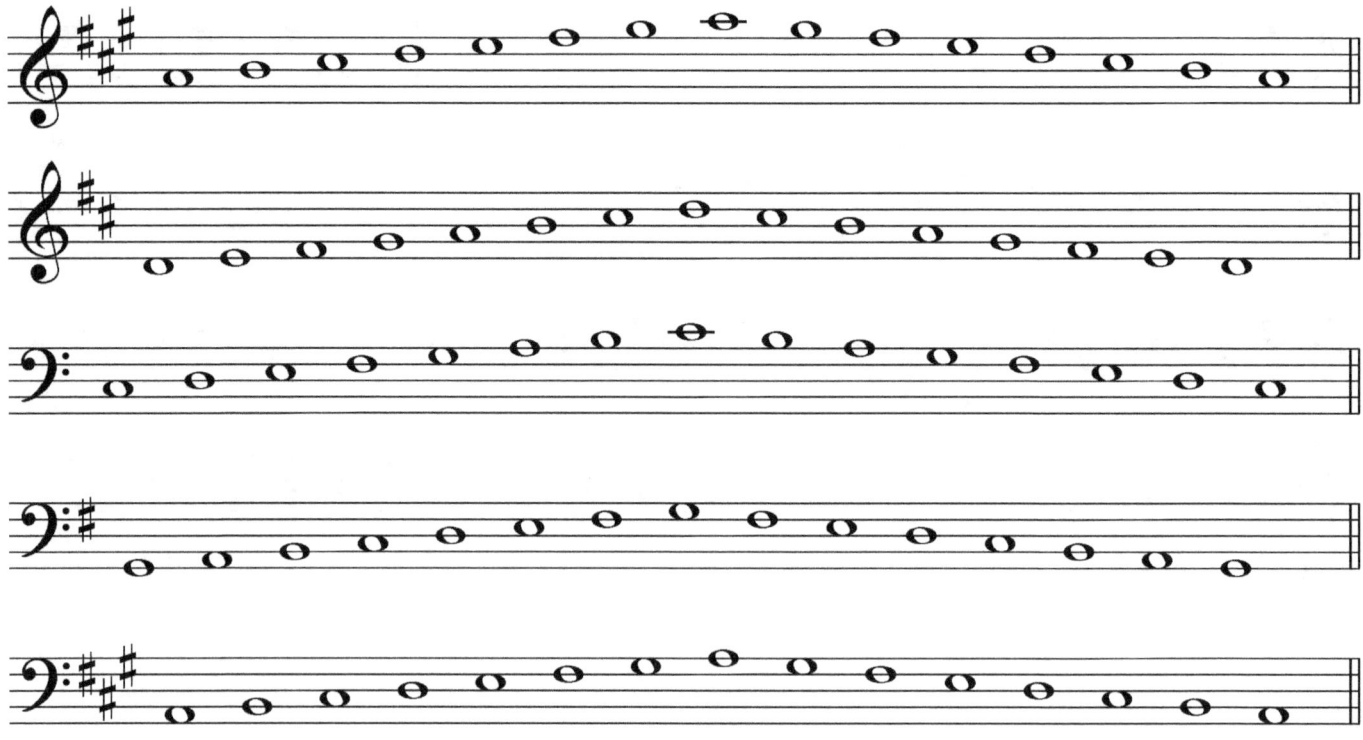

Page 59, No. 1

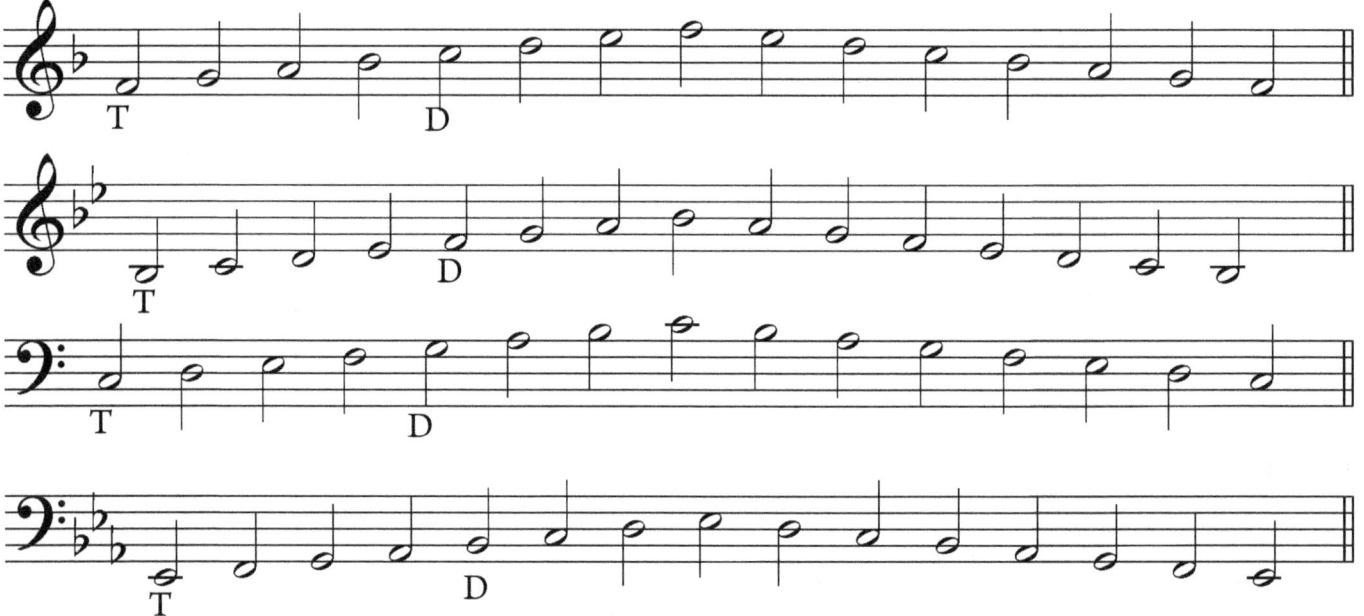

Page 60, No. 2 (other options for this question are possible)

Page 61, No. 3

Page 64, No. 1

Giuseppe Verdi
March from Aida

A♭ major

Gustav Mahler
Symphony No. 4, IV

E major

Francois Couperin
Concert Royal No. 2

D major

Franz Schubert
Waltz Op. 50

A major

Page 65, No. 2

Page 66, No. 1

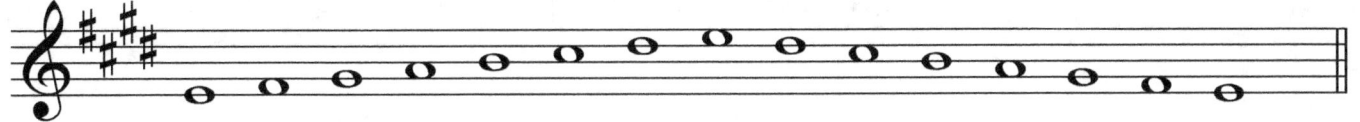

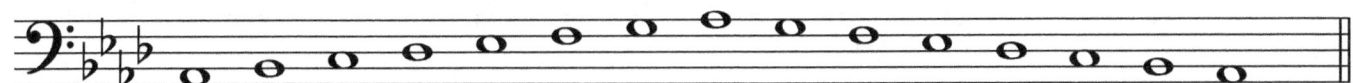

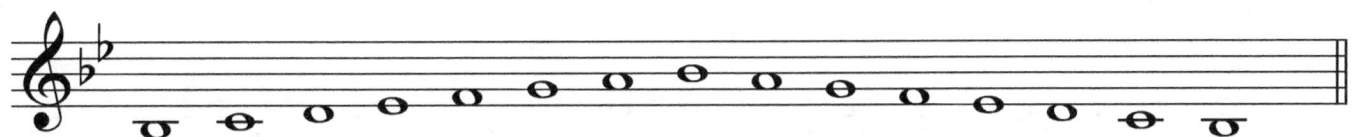

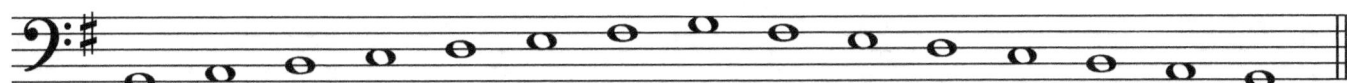

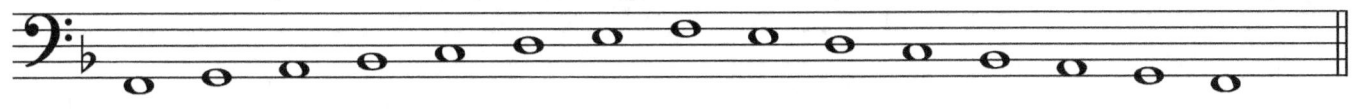

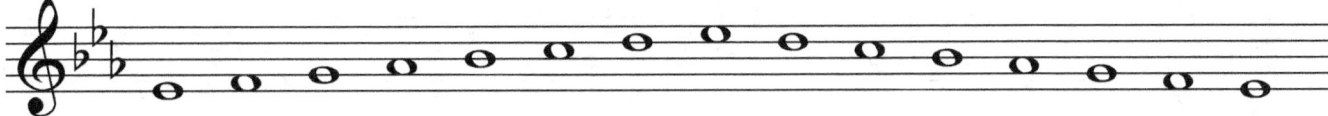

Page 67, No. 2

Page 68, No. 3

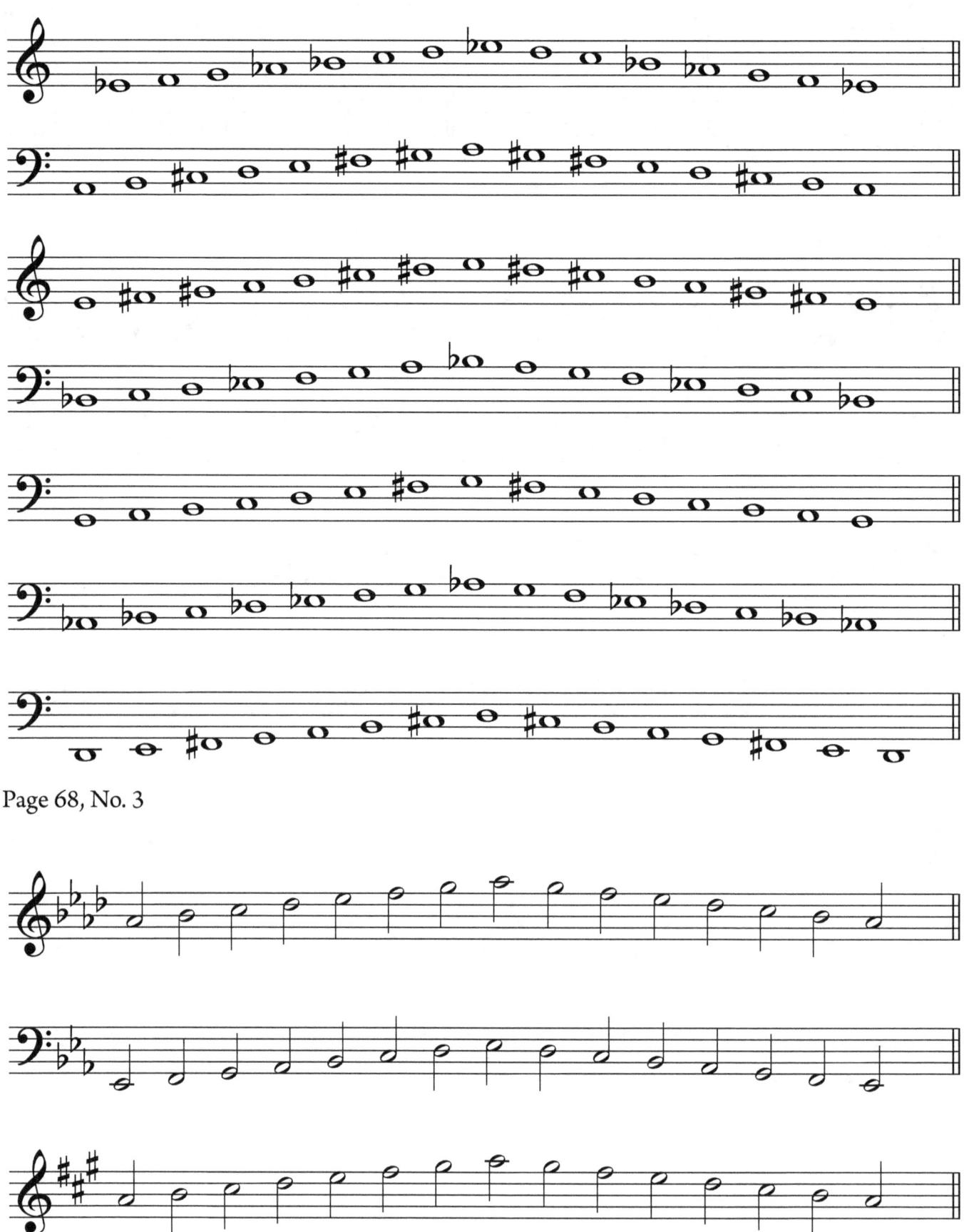

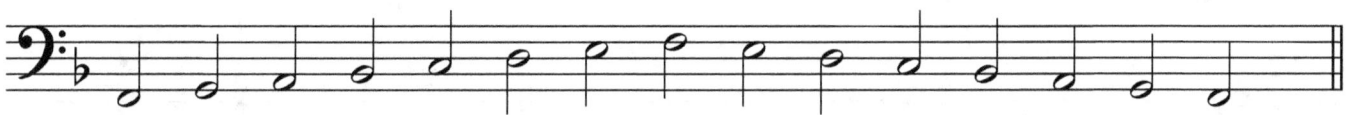

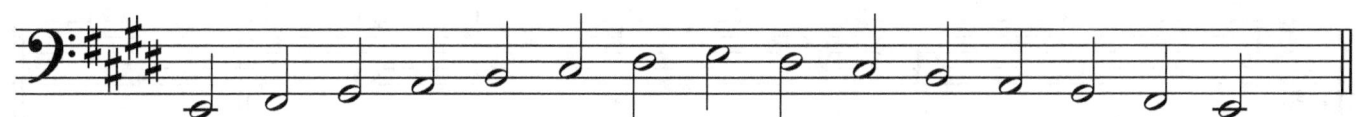

Page 72, No. 1

| | | | |
|---|---|---|---|
| C# | D | F# | |
| FCGDAEB | FC | FCGDAE | |
| G | A | B | E |
| F | FCG | FCGDA | FCGD |
| G♭ | A♭ | C♭ | |
| BEADGC | BEAD | BEADGCF | |
| B♭ | F | E♭ | D♭ |
| BE | B | BEA | BEADG |

Page 73, No. 1

Page 74, No. 2

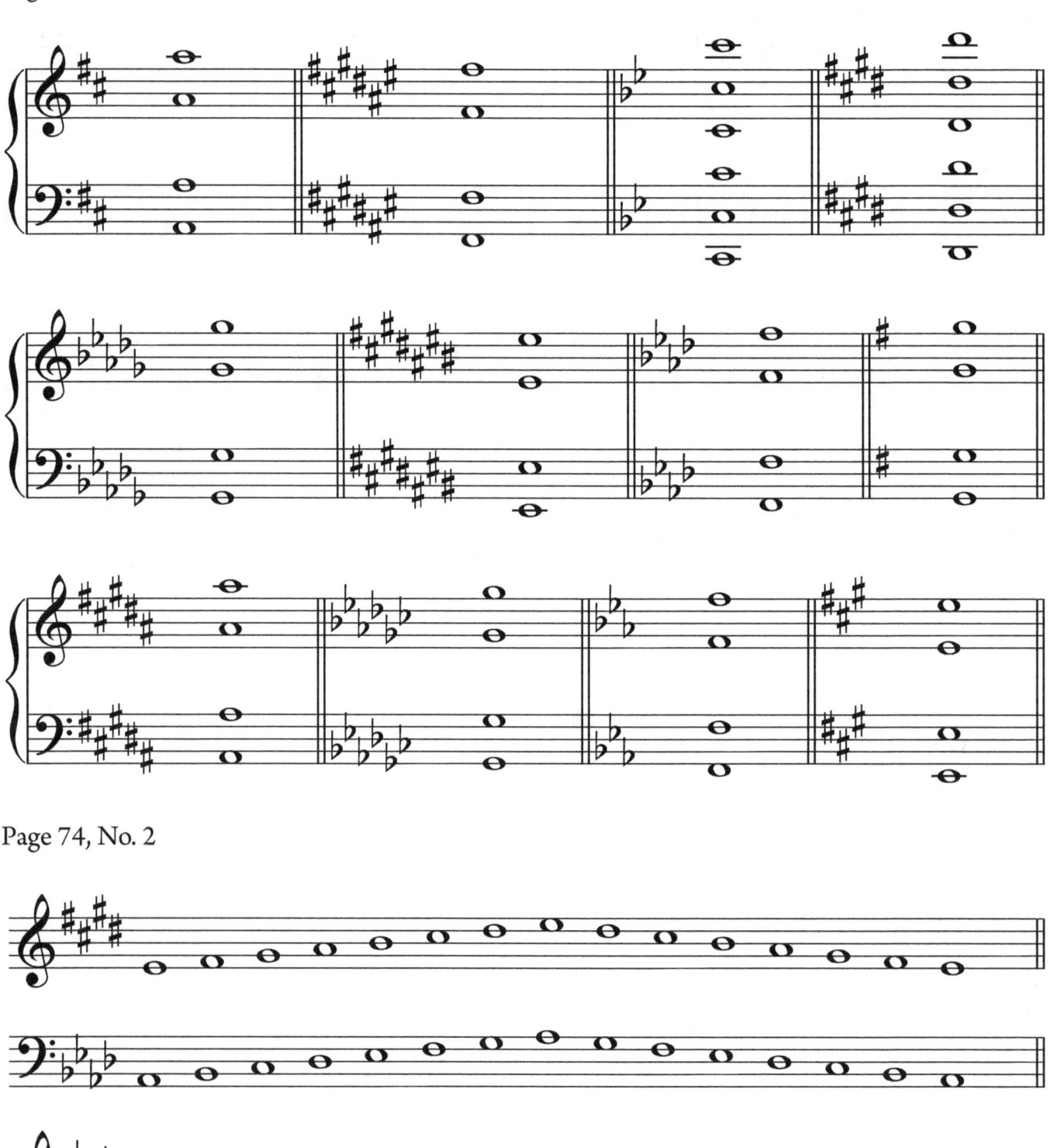

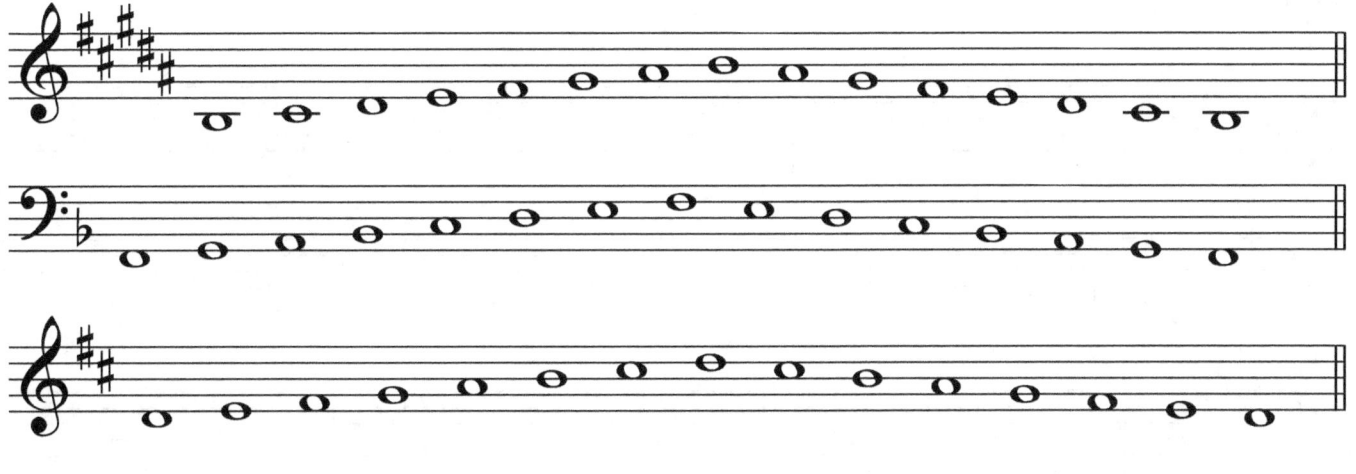

Page 75, No. 3 ( accidentals are not required descending)

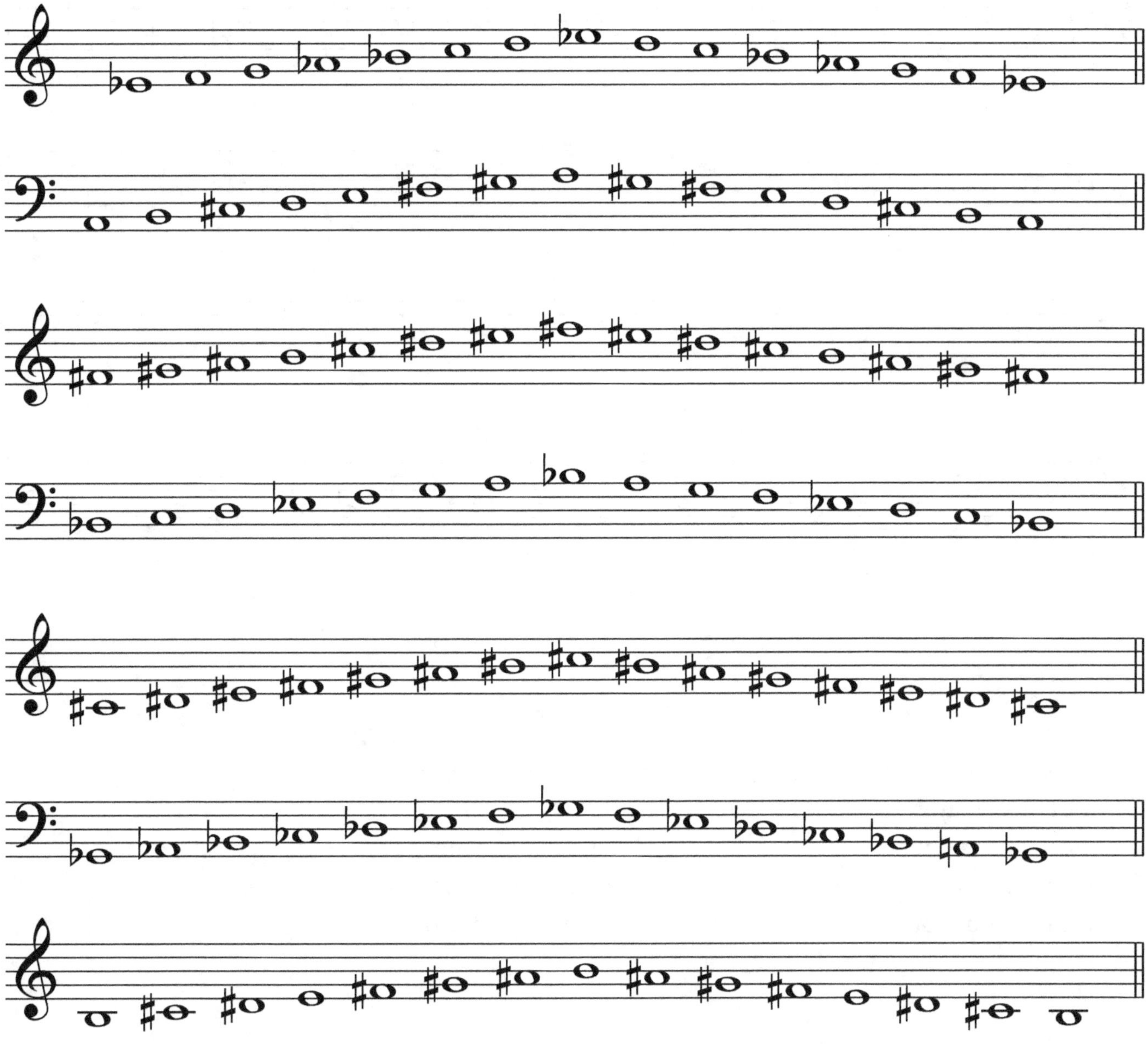

Page 76, No. 4

Page 79, No. 1

D minor    F major  
E minor    G major  
B minor    D major  
C minor    E♭ major  
F♯ minor   A major  

B♭ major   G minor  
C major    A minor  
D major    B minor  
E♭ major   C minor  
A major    F♯ minor

Page 81, No. 1

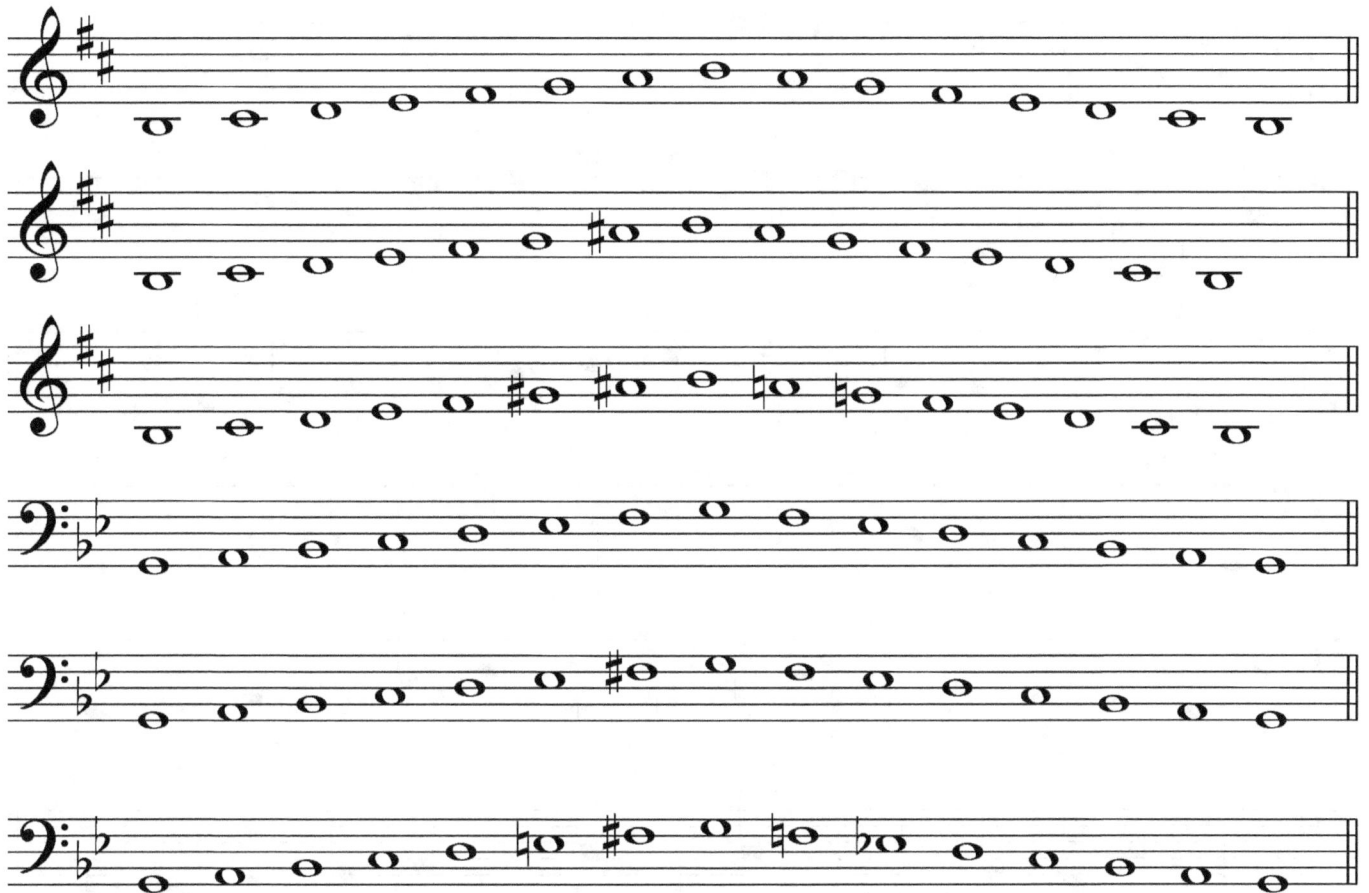

Page 82, No. 2

E natural minor
C harmonic minor
F# melodic minor
D harmonic minor
A harmonic minor
B harmonic minor
G melodic minor

Page 83, No. 3

Page 86, No. 1

E natural minor

B harmonic minor

C# harmonic minor

C melodic minor

F harmonic minor

A melodic minor

G natural minor

Page 87, No. 2

Page 88, No. 3

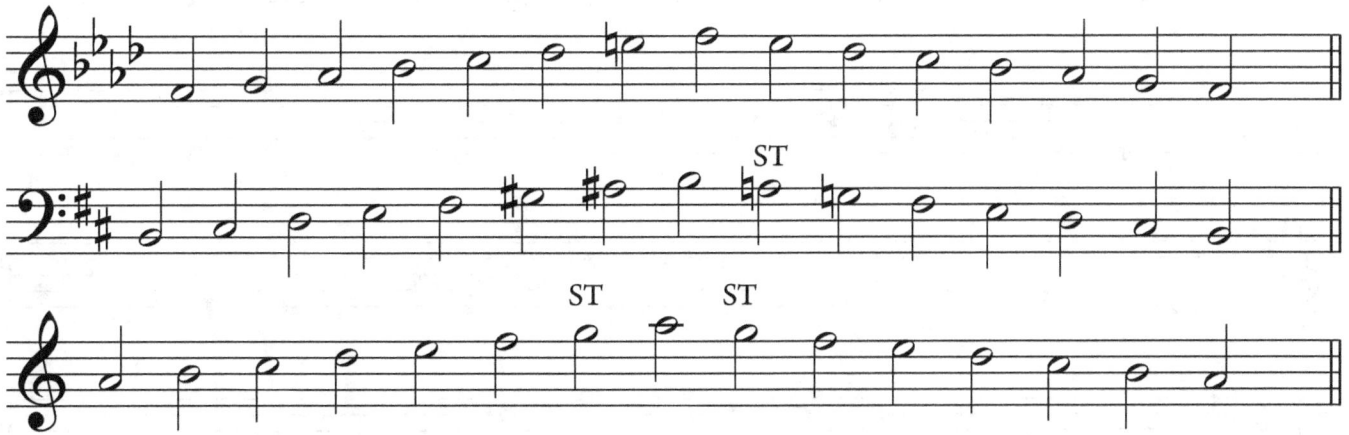

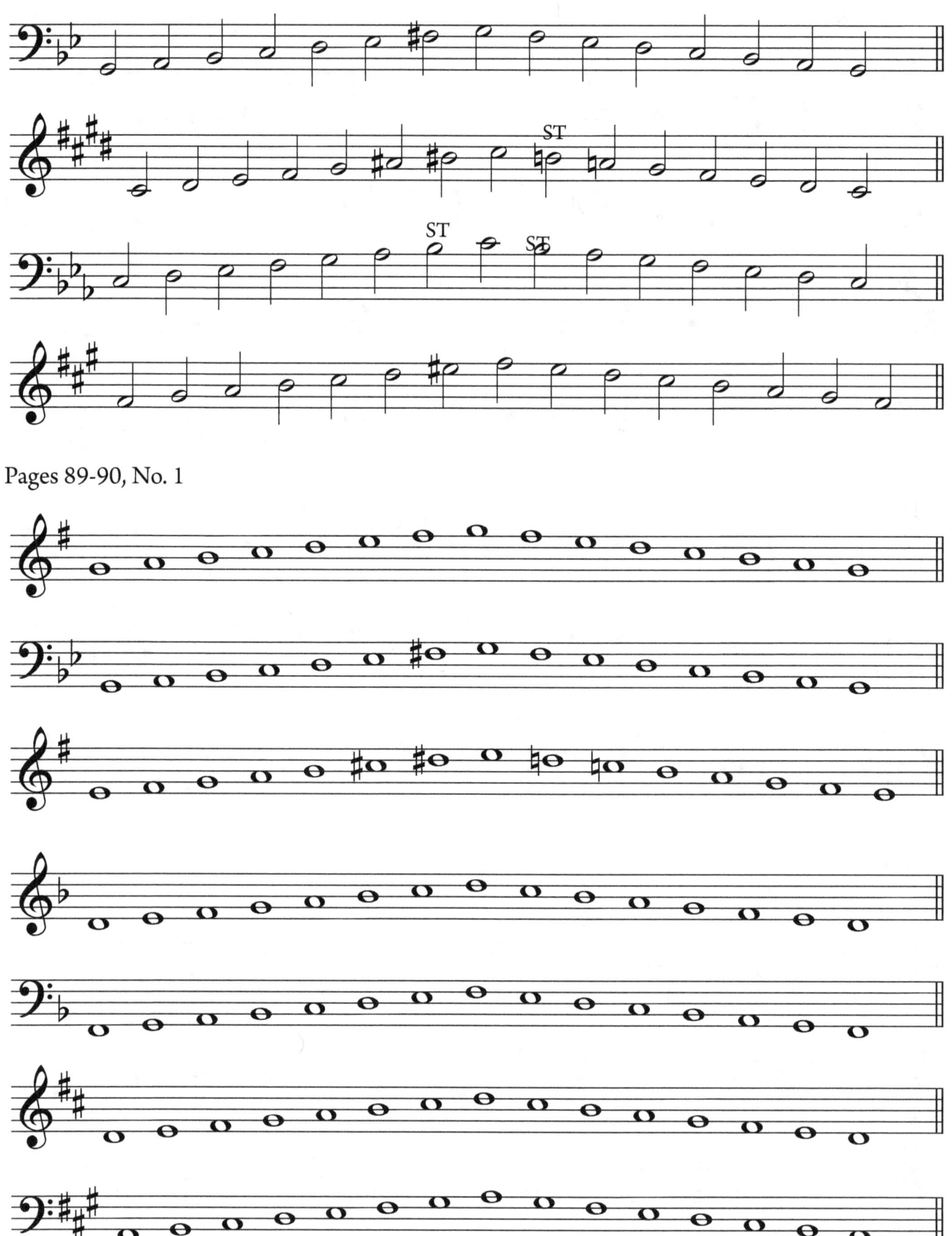

Pages 89-90, No. 1

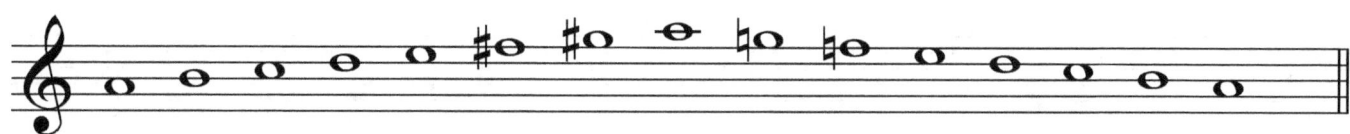

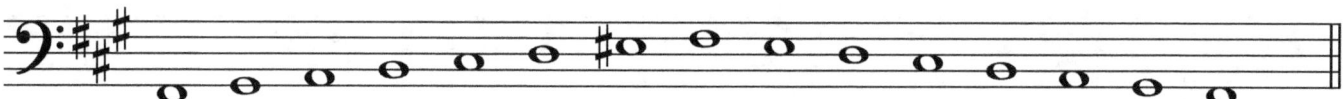

Page 92, No. 1

E♭ major
B♭ major
D minor
G minor
E minor
A♭ major
C minor

Page 94, No. 1

E natural minor
B♭ harmonic minor
G# harmonic minor
C melodic minor
D# harmonic minor
A melodic minor
G natural minor

Page 95, No. 2

Page 96, No. 1

a. The enharmonic tonic major of C♯ major is D♭ major.

b. The enharmonic tonic minor of B♭ major is A♯ minor.

c. The enharmonic tonic major of C♭ major is B major.

d. The parallel minor of D major is D minor.

e. The tonic major of G minor is G major.

f. The enharmonic tonic minor of E♭ major is D♯ minor.

Page 97, No. 2

Page 99, No. 1

per 5, maj 3, maj 6, maj 2, per 8, maj 7, maj 6

per 1, per 4, maj 6, maj 3, per 5, per 8, maj 2

Page 100, No. 1

Page 101, No. 1

Page 102, No. 2

maj 6, per 4, maj 3, min 7, min 7, min 6, per 5

maj 2, per 4, min 6, min 7, maj 3, maj 3, per 4

Page 103, No. 3

Page 103, No. 4

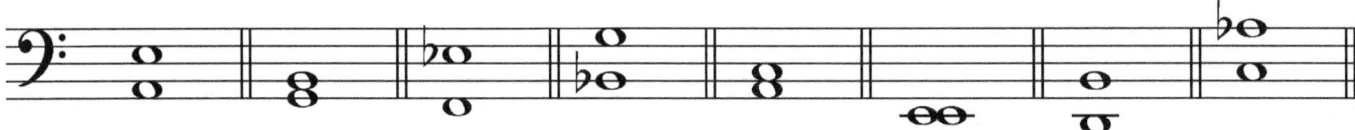

Page 104, No. 5

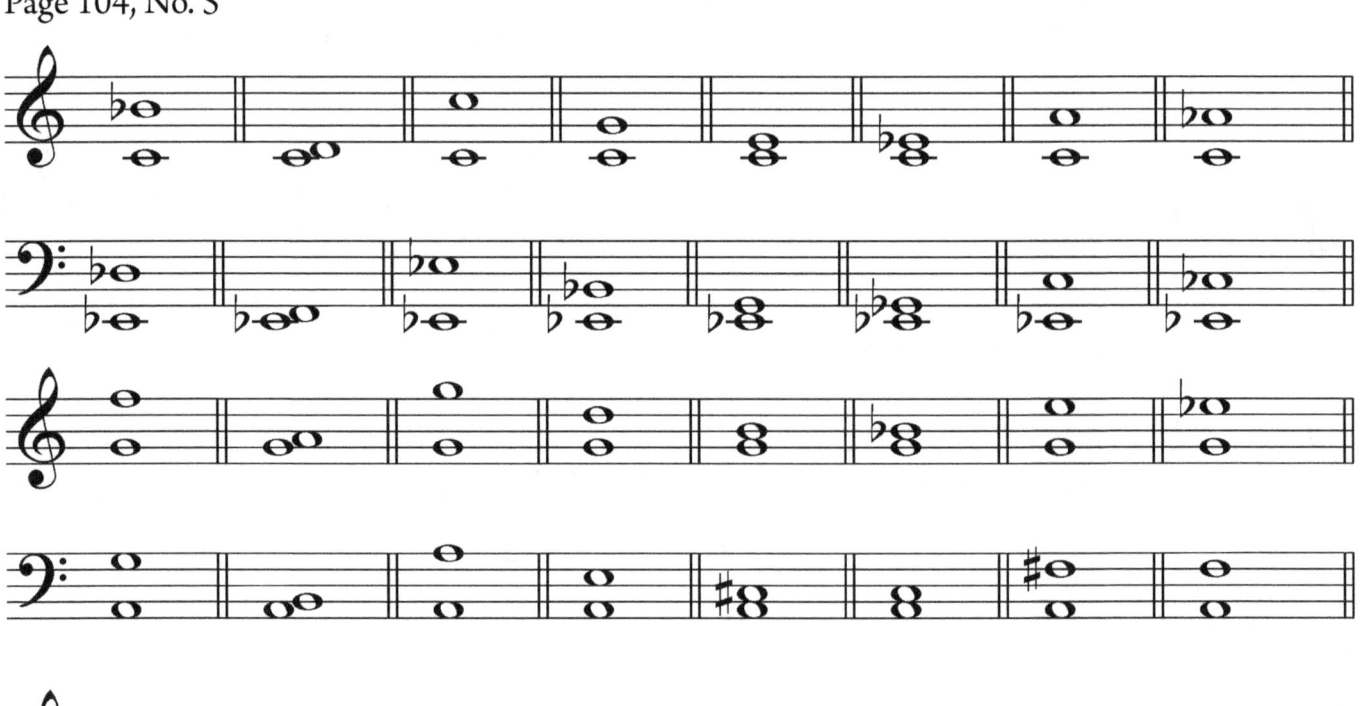

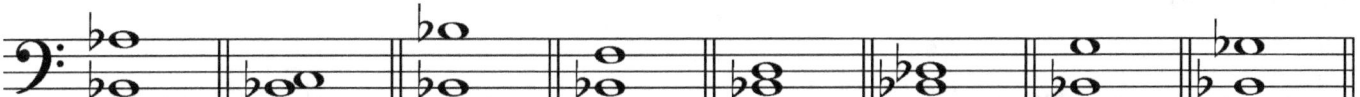

Page 105, No. 6

min 7,  maj 6

maj 2,  maj 2,  per 1

maj 3,  maj 2,  min 3,  min 3

per 5,  maj 2,  min 2,  maj 2,  min 2,  maj 2

Page 107, No. 1

Page 107, No. 2

Page 108, No. 1

Page 108, No. 2

Page 108, No. 3

CHS  DHS  DHS  CHS  CHS  DHS

DHS  CHS  DHS  CHS  CHS  DHS

CHS  DHS  DHS  CHS  DHS  DHS

DHS  CHS  CHS  DHS  CHS  DHS

Page 109, No. 1

Page 109, No. 2

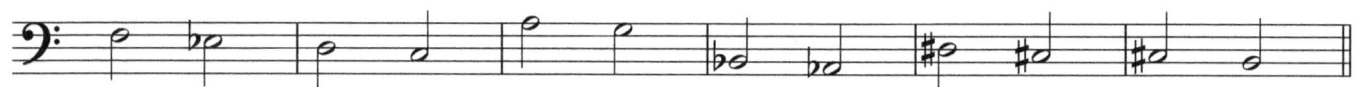

Page 110, No. 1

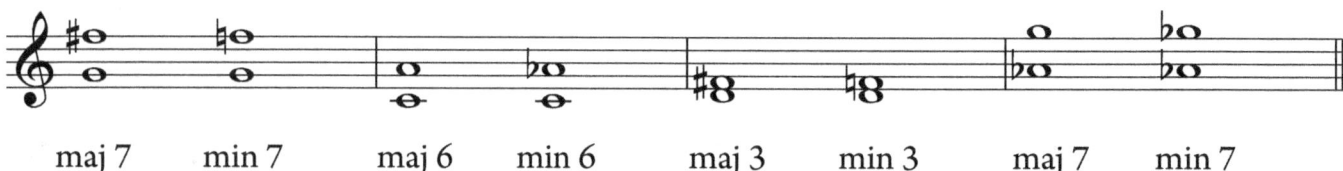

Page 110, No. 2

per 8   per 4   min 3   maj 2

per 5   per 4   maj 6   maj 3   min 2

Page 111, No. 3

per 5   min 3   per 4   maj 2   per 8   min 7   maj 7   per 5

per 5   min 6   per 5   min 6   min 7   maj 3   min 7   per 4

Page 111, No. 4

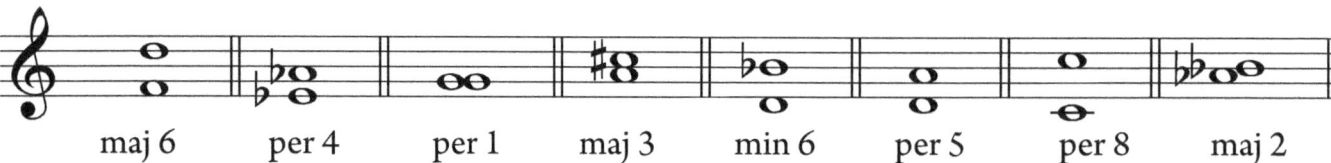

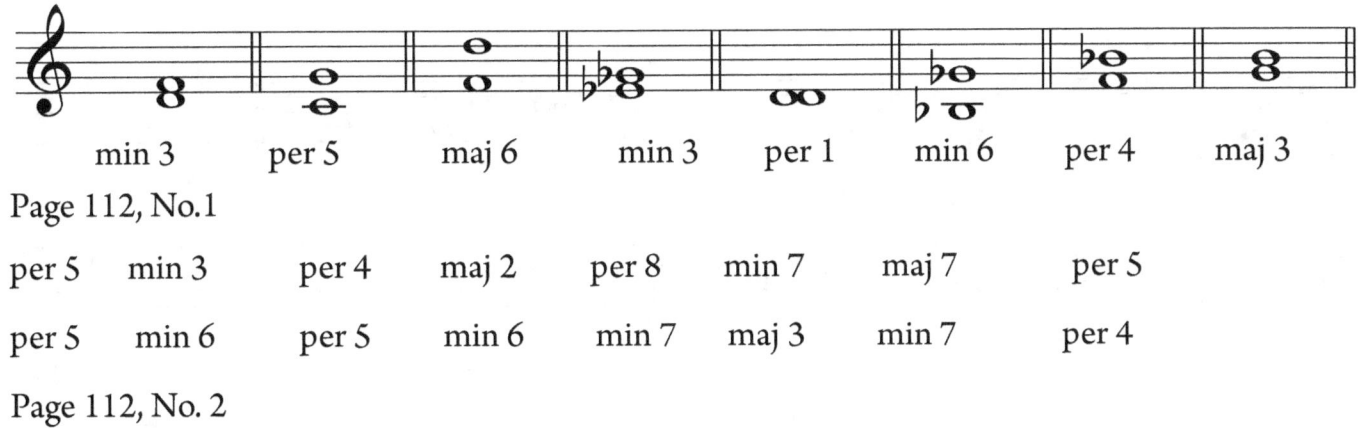

Page 112, No.1

| per 5 | min 3 | per 4 | maj 2 | per 8 | min 7 | maj 7 | per 5 |
| per 5 | min 6 | per 5 | min 6 | min 7 | maj 3 | min 7 | per 4 |

Page 112, No. 2

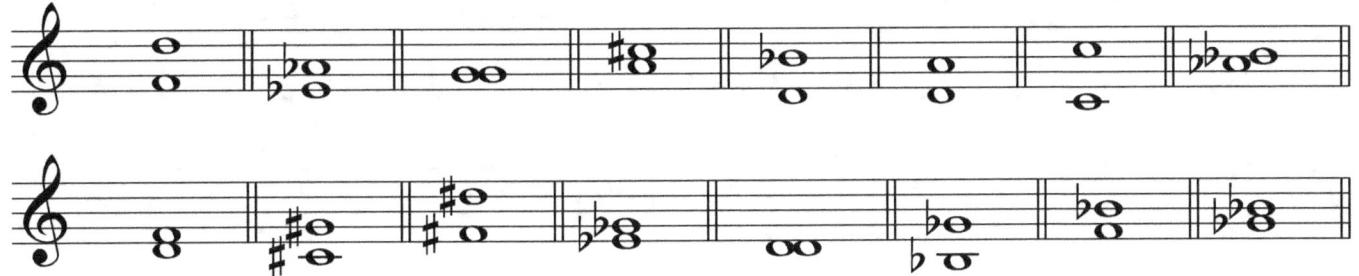

Page 113, No. 1

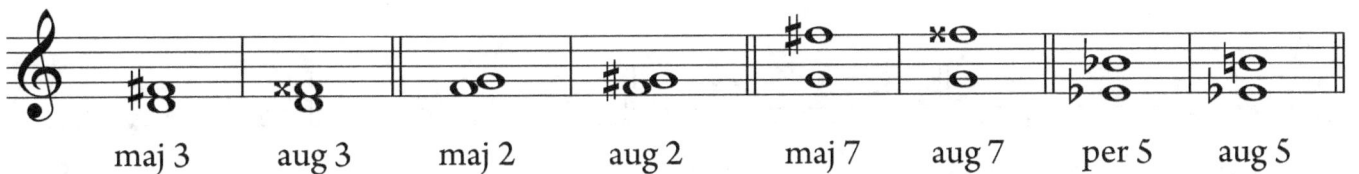

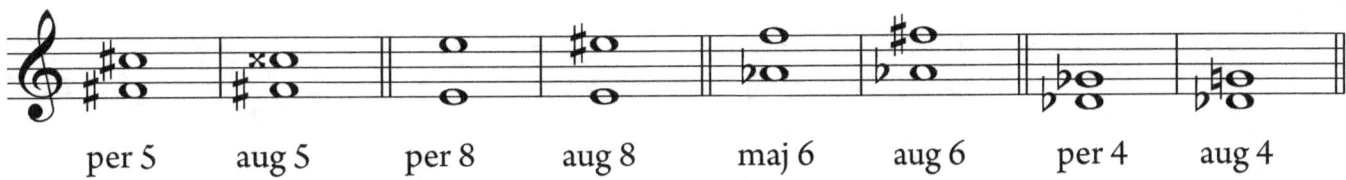

Page 114, No. 2

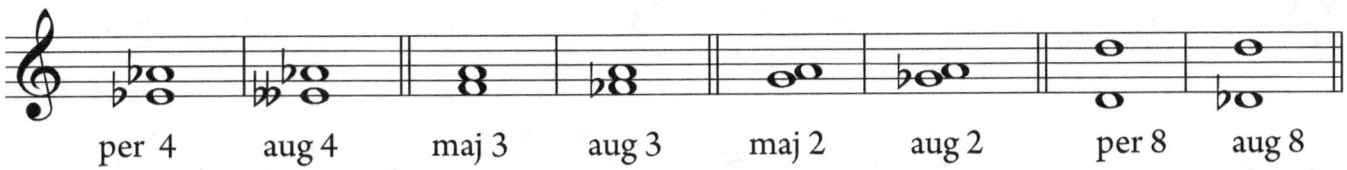

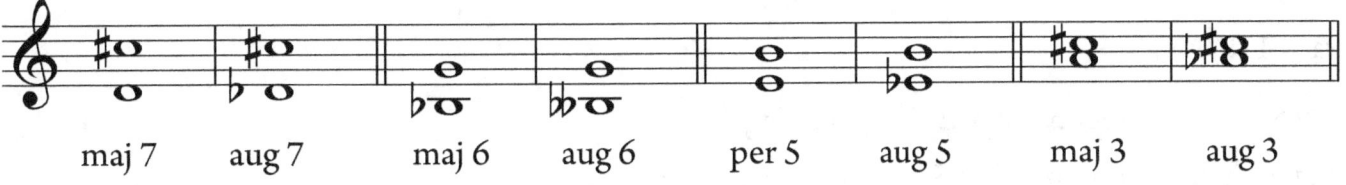

Page 118, No. 4

aug 5   min 6   per 5   maj 2   aug 3   aug 4

maj 3   per 8   dim 6   dim 5   dim 2   per 1

Page 118, No. 5

maj 2    dim 4    per 5    per 8    maj 3    min 2    min 3    maj 2

Page 118, No. 6

Page 120, No. 1

per 5    dim 3    maj 6    min 7    aug 2    dim 5

Page 120, No. 2

per 4    aug 5    aug 2    dim 7    dim 7    min 7

Page 120, No. 3

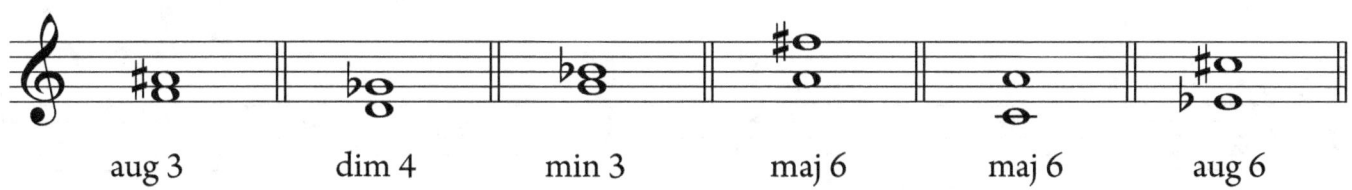

aug 3         dim 4         min 3         maj 6         maj 6         aug 6

Page 120, No. 4

min 6    min 2    per 4    maj 3
per 4    per 4    min 3    min 3    per 4
per 4    per 4    min 2    maj 2    min 3
maj 2    dim 5    min 2    min 3    per 4

Page 124, No. 1

Page 125, No. 2

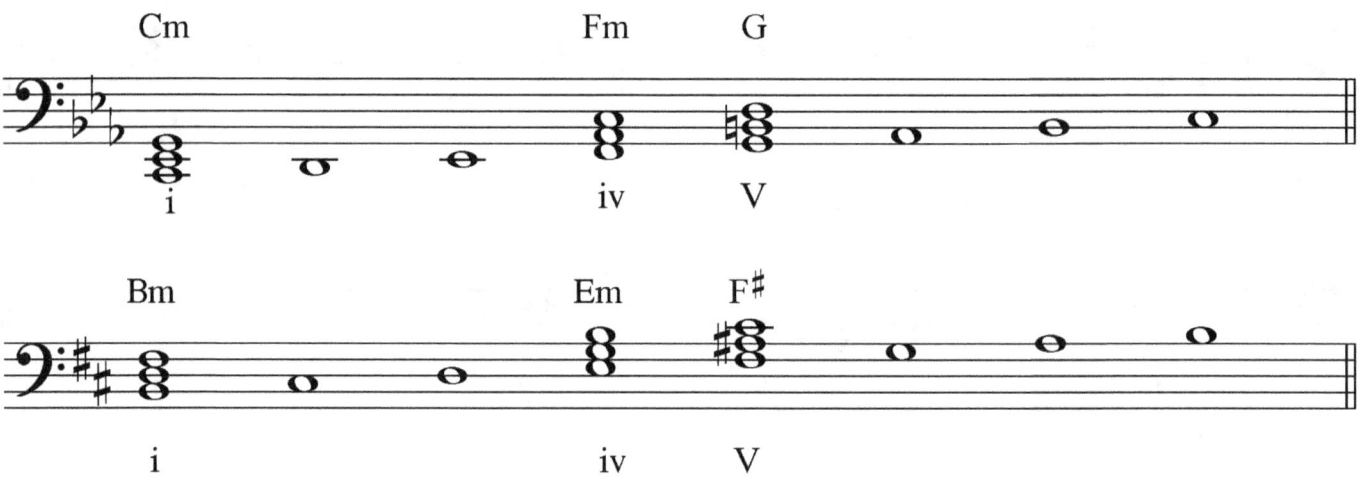

Page 128, No. 2

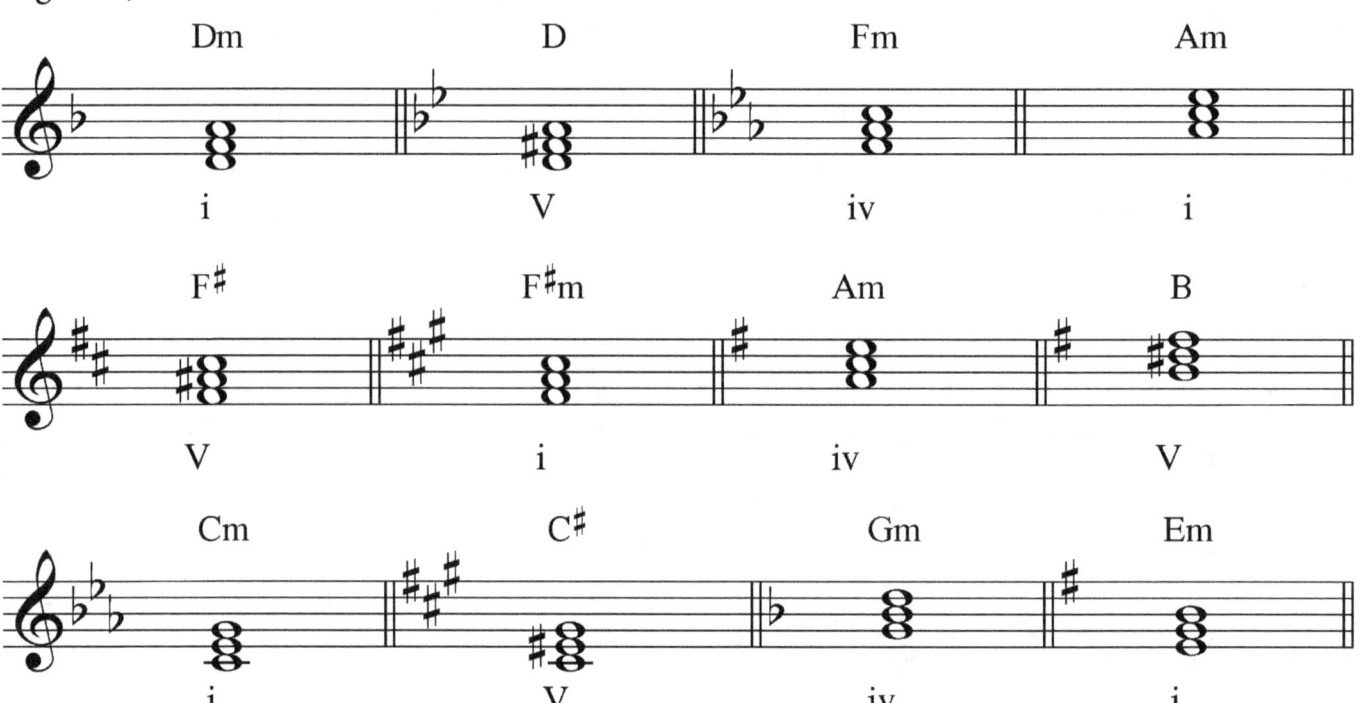

Page 128, No. 3

| Key:   | E minor | G minor     | F# minor    | C minor |
|--------|---------|-------------|-------------|---------|
| Triad: | tonic   | dominant    | subdominant | tonic   |
|        | i       | V           | iv          | i       |

| Key:   | B minor   | D minor     | F# minor | C minor  |
|--------|-----------|-------------|----------|----------|
| Triad: | dominant  | subdominant | tonic    | dominant |
|        | V         | iv          | i        | V        |

Page 131, No. 1

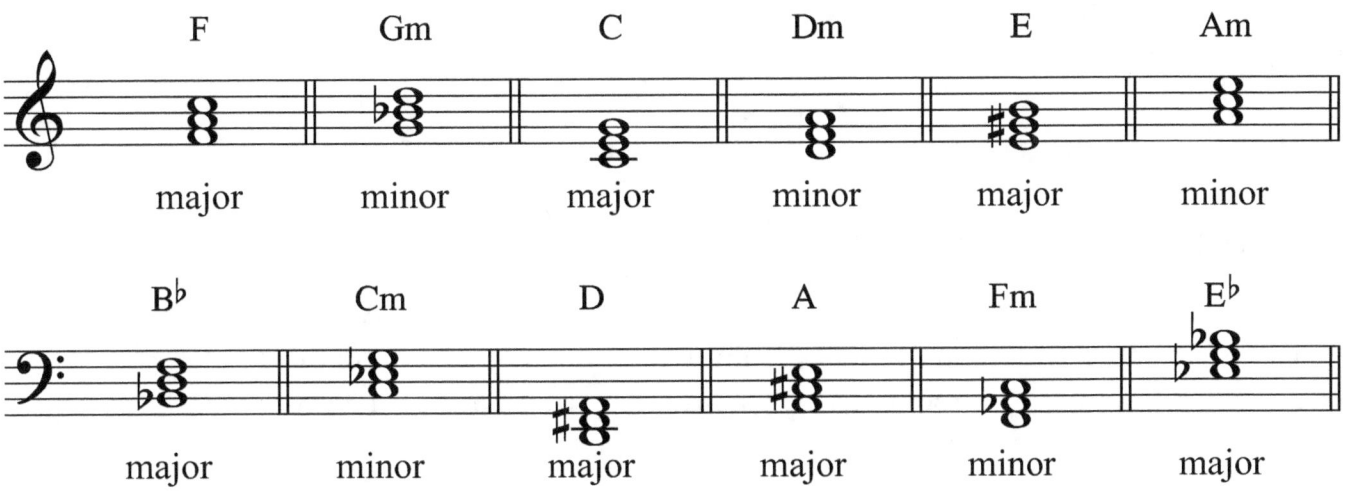

Page 131, No. 2

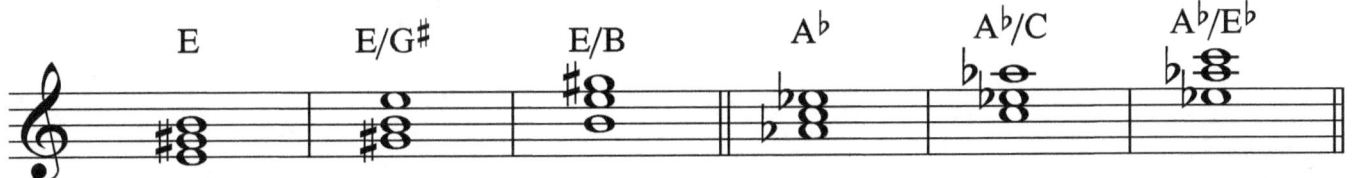

Page 132, No. 3

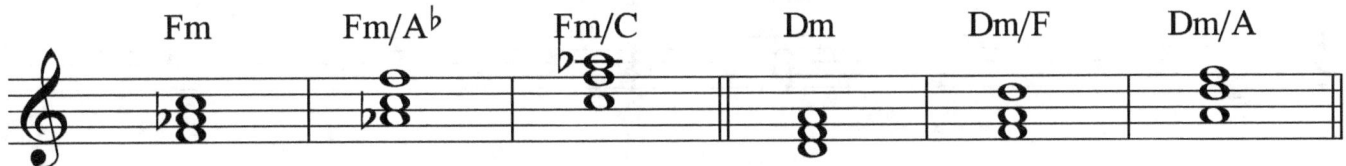

Page 133, No. 1

B♭ C E G D D
F E♭ D E C A

Page 133, No. 2

| E | F | G | D | A | A |
|---|---|---|---|---|---|
| minor | minor | major | minor | major | minor |
| 2nd inv | 1st inv. | root pos. | 1st inv. | root pos. | 1st inv. |

| B♭ | A♭ | B | G | E | F |
|---|---|---|---|---|---|
| major | major | minor | minor | minor | major |
| 1st inv. | root pos. | 2nd inv. | root pos. | 2nd inv. | root pos. |

Page 135, No. 1

46

Page 135, No. 2

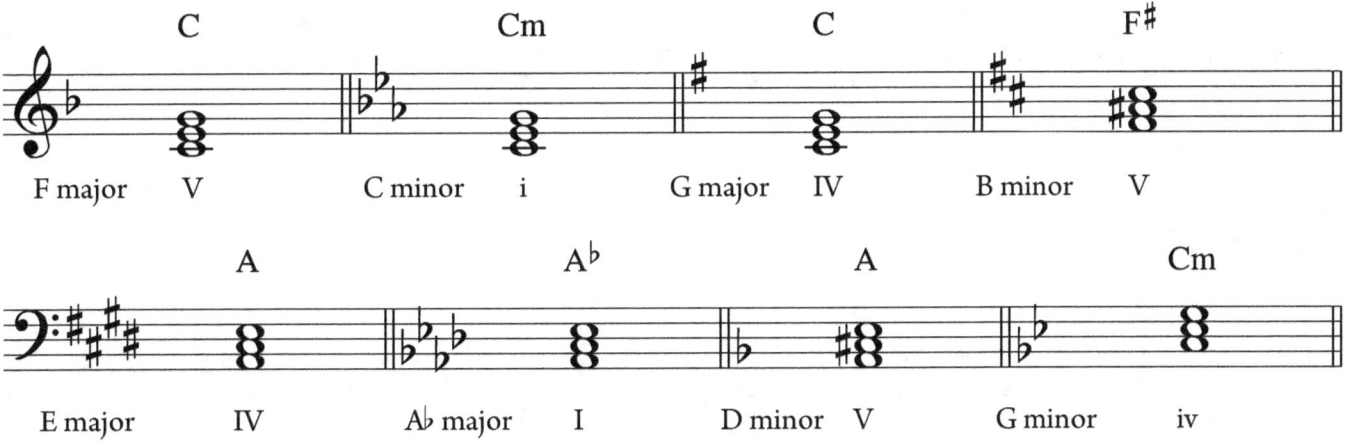

Page 136, No. 3

Page 136, No. 4

Page 138, No. 1

D major   G major   C major   F major   B♭ major   E♭ major

Page 138, No. 2

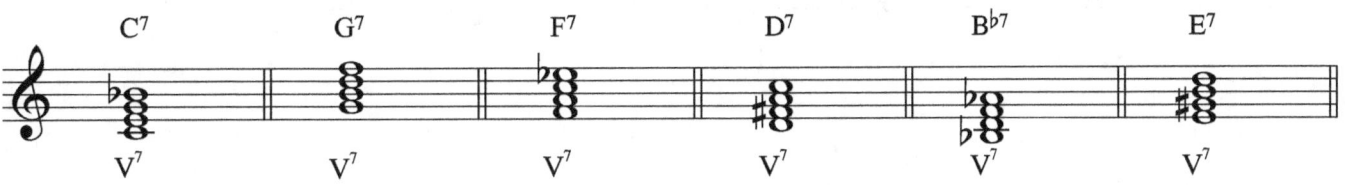

Page 138, No. 3

Page 138, No. 4

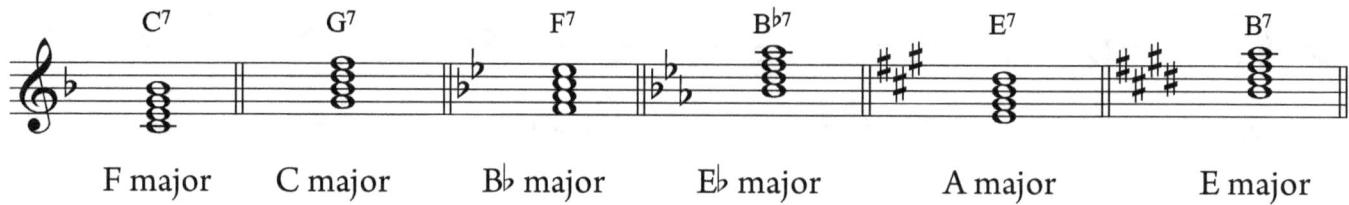

Page 139, No. 1

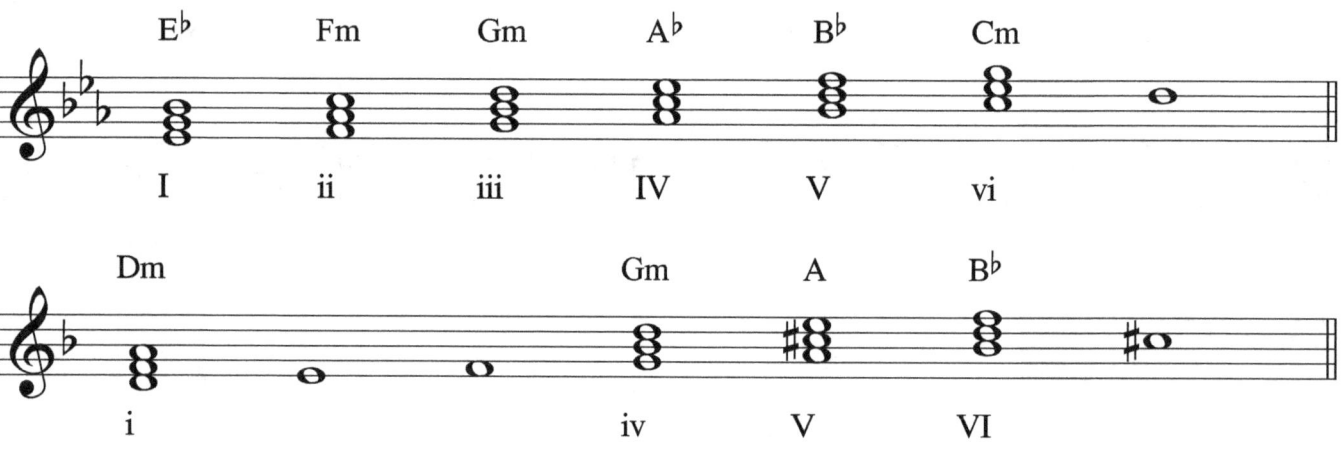

Page 140, No. 2

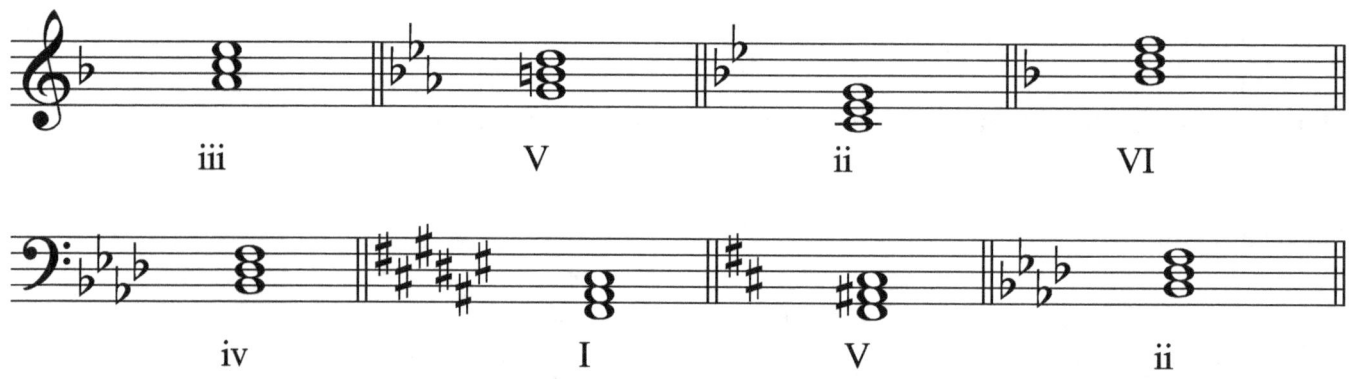

Page 140, No. 3

Page 141, No. 1

| C | B♭ | E | G | A | E♭ |
|---|---|---|---|---|---|
| minor | major | major | major | minor | major |
| root pos | 1st inv | root pos | root pos | 1st inv | 2nd inv |

| C♯ | F | B | G♭ | E | F♯ |
|---|---|---|---|---|---|
| major | minor | major | major | minor | minor |
| root pos | root pos | 2nd inv | 2nd inv | 2nd inv | 2nd inv |

Page 142, No. 2

| F major | D major | E♭ major | G major | B major | A major |
|---|---|---|---|---|---|
| F minor | D minor | E♭ minor | G minor | B minor | A minor |

Page 144-145, No. 1

| A major: | A | D | A | |
|---|---|---|---|---|
| | major | major | major | |
| | root pos | root pos | root pos | |
| | $\hat{1}$ | $\hat{4}$ | $\hat{1}$ | |

| C major: | C | G | A | D |
|---|---|---|---|---|
| | major | major | minor | minor |
| | root pos | 1st inv | root pos | 1st inv |
| | $\hat{1}$ | $\hat{5}$ | $\hat{6}$ | $\hat{2}$ |

| A minor: | A | E | | |
|---|---|---|---|---|
| | minor | major | | |
| | root pos | root pos | | |
| | $\hat{1}$ | $\hat{5}$ | | |

| G major: | G | D | | |
|---|---|---|---|---|
| | major | major | | |
| | root pos | 1st inv | | |
| | $\hat{1}$ | $\hat{5}$ | | |

| E minor: | E | B | | |
|---|---|---|---|---|
| | minor | major | | |
| | root pos | root pos | | |
| | $\hat{1}$ | $\hat{5}$ | | |

Page 149-150, No. 1

|  |  |  |  |  |  |
|---|---|---|---|---|---|
|  | E | A |  | F | B♭ |
|  | V | I |  | V | I |
| A major: | perfect authentic | | B♭ major: | imperfect authentic | |

|  |  |  |  |  |  |
|---|---|---|---|---|---|
|  | G | C |  | G | Cm |
|  | V | I |  | V | i |
| C major: | perfect authentic | | C minor: | imperfect authentic | |

|  |  |  |  |  |  |
|---|---|---|---|---|---|
|  | B | E |  | A | Dm |
|  | V | I |  | V | i |
| E major: | perfect authentic | | D minor: | perfect authentic | |

|  |  |  |  |  |  |
|---|---|---|---|---|---|
|  | F | B♭m |  | B | Em |
|  | V | i |  | V | i |
| B♭ minor: | imperfect authentic | | E minor: | perfect authentic | |

Page 152, No. 1

Page 153, No. 1

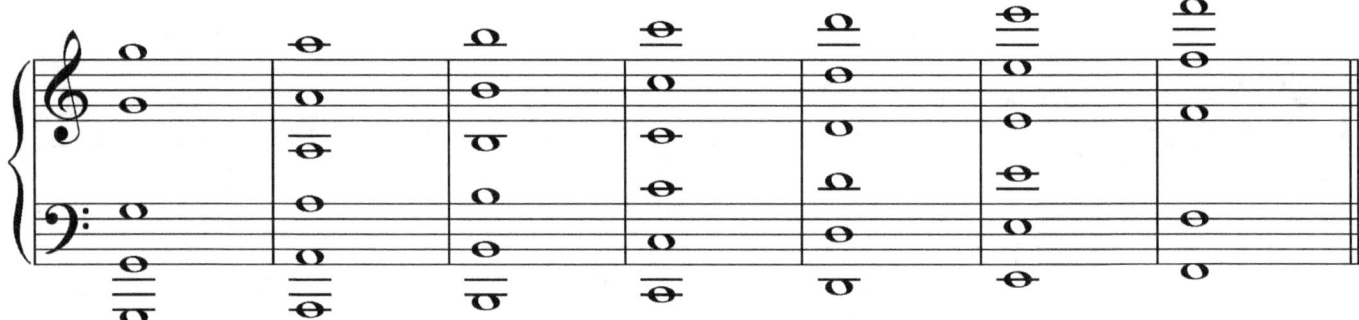

Page 153, No. 2

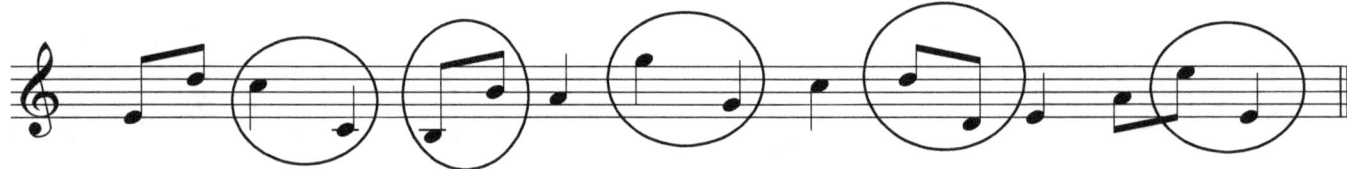

Page 155, No. 1

Page 156, No. 2

Page 156, No. 3

Ludwig van Beethoven
Leonore, No. 2

Enrique Granados
Spanish Dance, No. 6

Page 157, No. 4

Page 158, No. 5

Page 158, No. 6

Page 161, No. 1

Page 162, No. 2

Key: E♭ major

Key: G major

Key: B♭ major

Key: C major

Key: D♭ major

Page 164, No. 1

F major

Page 165, No. 1

Page 166, No. 2

Page 169, No. 1 (other options are possible)

Page 169, No. 2 (other options are possible)

Page 169, No. 3 (other options are possible)

Page 170, No. 4 (other options are possible)

Page 170, No. 5 (other options are possible)

Page 170, No. 6 (other options are possible)

Page 172, No. 1

key: F major

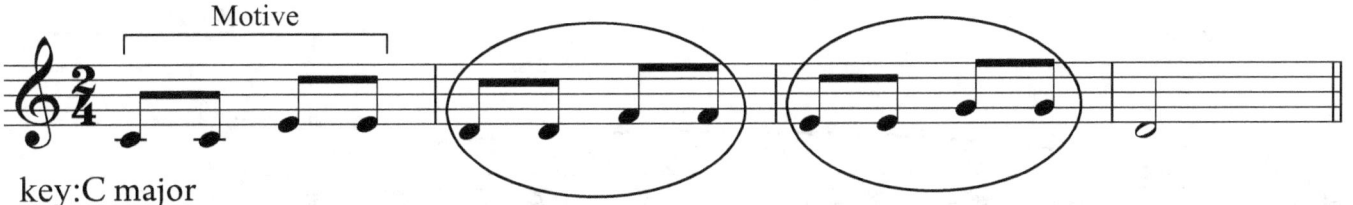

key: C major

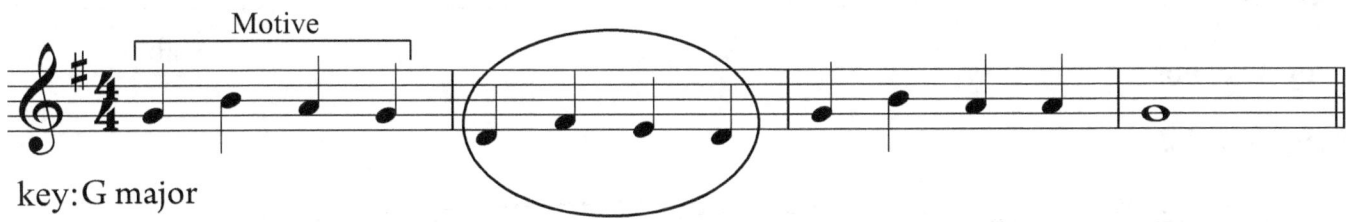

key: G major

Page 172, No. 2

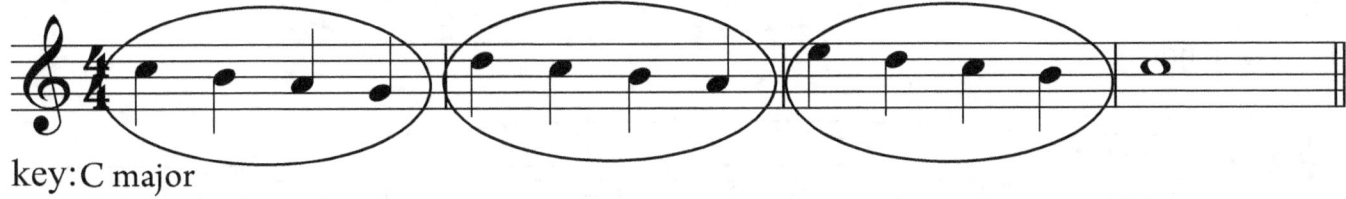

key: C major

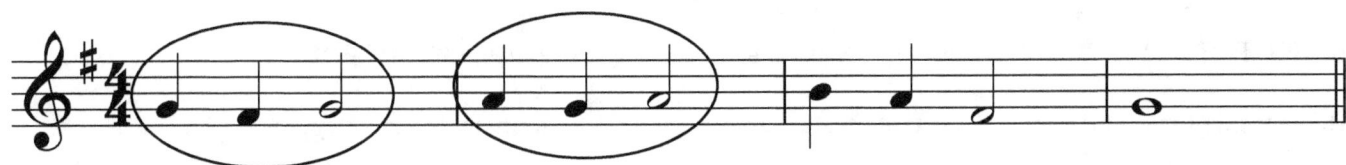

key: G major

Page 176, No. 2

key: F major

The first phrase ends on:   ☐ a stable scale degree   ☑ an unstable scale degree
The second phrase ends on:  ☑ a stable scale degree   ☐ an unstable scale degree
This is a:                  ☐ parallel period          ☑ contrasting period

Page 177-178, No. 1 (other options are possible)

Page 182, No. 1

Page 185, No. 1

Page 186, No. 1

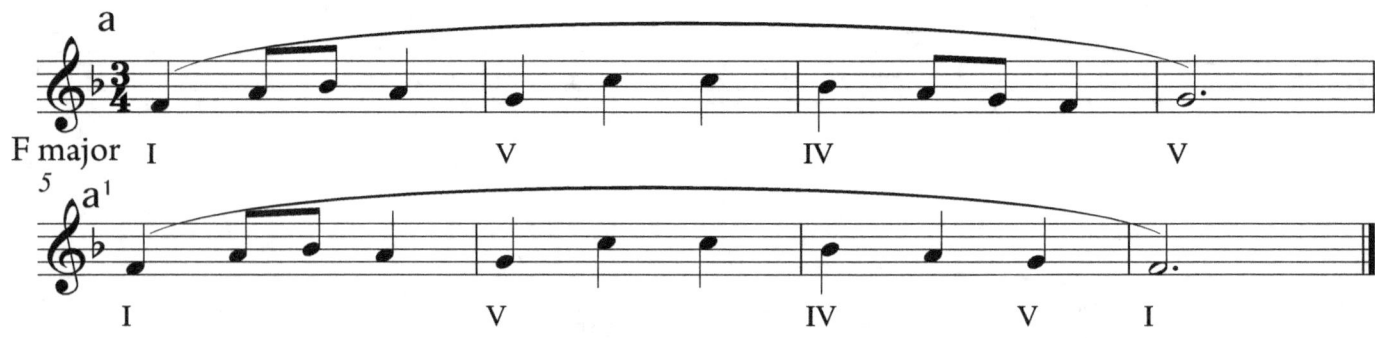

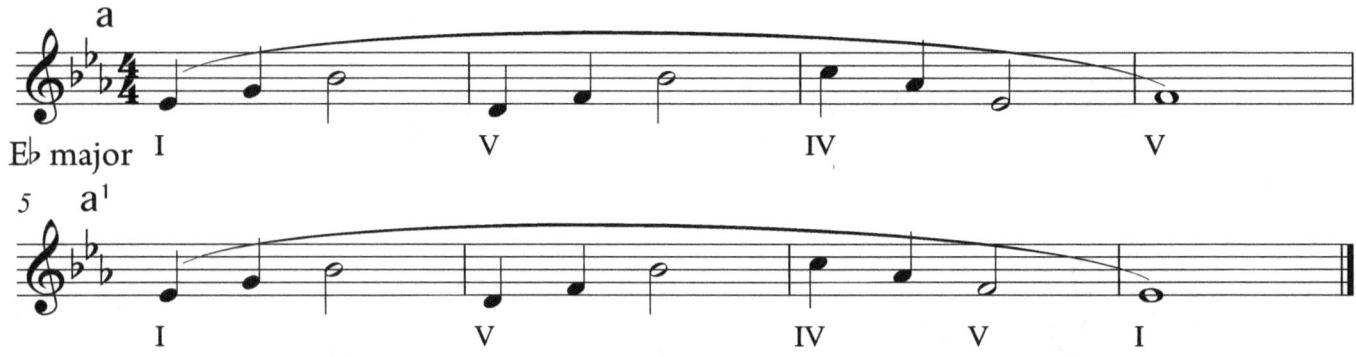

Page 201

a. Who composed Young Persons Guide to the Orchestra? **Benjamin Britten**
b. In what country was he born? **England or Great Britain**
c. In what era did he live? **Modern**
d. Who composed the theme on which this work is based? **Henry Purcell**
e. What era did this composer live? **Baroque**
f. How many variations are in Young Persons Guide to the Orchestra? **13**
g. What are the four instrument families featured in this composition?

    1. **Strings**
    2. **Woodwinds**
    3. **Brass**
    4. **Percussion**

h. What type of piece is the final movement of this composition? **Fugue**

Page 215

a) Germany
b) Baroque
c) England
d) A large composition for orchestra, choir and soloists based on a religious theme.
e) 1741
f) Soprano   Alto   Tenor   Bass
g) Technique of writing music that mirrors the meaning of a piece.
h) The text "Forever and ever" is repeated over and over.
i) An opera is a play with music.
j) Classical era
k) 1791
l) Singspiel
m) German
n) A song in an opera that can be taken out and sung in a musical performance.
o) Coloratura

Page 216

☑ Harold Arlen
☑ American
☑ Judy Garland
☑ AABA

Page 224

| | | | | |
|---|---|---|---|---|
| a. The Baroque period occurred approximately: | ☐ | 1600-1700 | ☐ | 1650-1725 |
| | ☐ | 2010-2015 | ☑ | 1600-1750 |

| | | | | |
|---|---|---|---|---|
| b. The following are famous Baroque composers: | ☑ | J.S. Bach | ☑ | Vivaldi |
| | ☐ | Mozart | ☑ | Handel |

| | | | | |
|---|---|---|---|---|
| c. These elements can be used to describe Baroque music: | ☑ | counterpoint | ☑ | doctrine of affections |
| | ☐ | romantic | ☑ | highly ornamented |

| | | | | |
|---|---|---|---|---|
| d. These are Bach's 3 main periods. | ☑ | Leipzig | ☑ | Weimar |
| | ☐ | Berlin | ☑ | Cöthen |

| | | | | |
|---|---|---|---|---|
| e. Bach composed for the following mediums. | ☑ | keyboard | ☑ | orchestra |
| | ☑ | choir | ☑ | chamber music |

| | | | | |
|---|---|---|---|---|
| f. How many 2 part inventions did J.S. Bach write? | ☐ | 21 | ☑ | 15 |
| | ☐ | 12 | ☐ | 6 |

| | | | | |
|---|---|---|---|---|
| g. The 3-part inventions are also known as: | ☐ | sonatas | ☑ | sinfonias |
| | ☐ | dances | ☐ | fugues |

| | | | | |
|---|---|---|---|---|
| h. The 2-part inventions are written for this many voices: | ☑ | 2 | ☐ | 3 |
| | ☐ | 6 | ☐ | 32 |

| | | | | |
|---|---|---|---|---|
| i. 3 elements found in the 2-part inventions are: | ☑ | motives | ☑ | sequence |
| | ☑ | imitation | ☐ | monophony |

| | | | | |
|---|---|---|---|---|
| j. This is the numbering system used to identify Bach's works: | ☐ | NRA | ☑ | BWV |
| | ☐ | BVW | ☐ | BMW |

Page 225

a. Who composed Brandenburg Concerto No. 5? **Johann Sebastian Bach**

b. What genre is this work? **concerto grosso**

c. What 3 instruments are featured in this work? **violin, flute, harpsichord**

d. What is this group of instruments called? **concertino**

e. The full string orchestra in a concerto grosso is called a

☑ ripieno ☐ concertino ☐ oratorio ☐ sequence

f. The form of the first movement of Brandenburg Concerto No. 5 is

☐ rondo ☑ ritornello ☐ sonata ☐ binary

a. T
b. F
c. T
d. F
e. T
f. F
g. T
h. T
i. F
j. T

Page 229, No. 1

Franz Schubert
Slumber Song

a. Add the time signature directly on the music.

b. Name the key of this piece. **G major**

c. Mark the phrases with slurs.

d. Label the phrases with *a*, *a¹*, and *b*.

e. Name the chord formed by the notes at A: **G major**  B: **D major**

# Piano Sonata, Mvt. I

Franz Joseph Haydn
(1732-1809)

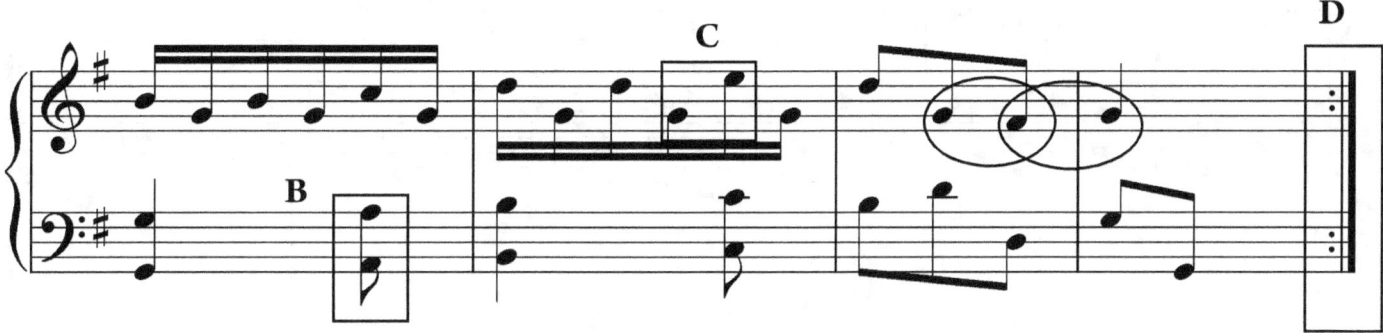

a. Add the correct time signature directly on the music.

b. Name the key of this piece. **G major**

c. Name the composer of this piece. **Franz Joseph Haydn**

d. On which beat does this piece begin? **3**

e. Name the intervals at : A **maj 3**  B **per 8**  C **maj 6**

f. Does this piece end on a stable or unstable degree? **stable**

g. Explain the sign at D. **Repeat sign, repeat from the beginning**

h. Define *Presto* **Very fast**

i. Find one half step and circle it.

## Menuetto

Wolfgang Amadeus Mozart
(1756-1791)

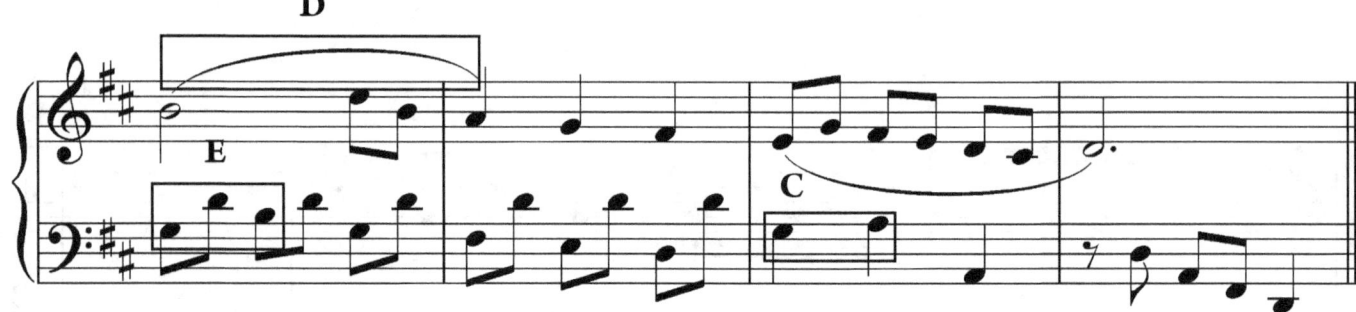

a. Add the correct time signature directly on the music.

b. Name the key of this piece. **D major**

c. Name the composer of this piece. **Wolfgang Amadeus Mozart**

d. When did this composer live? **1756-1791**

e. Name the intervals at : A **per 4**  B  **per 5**  C **maj 2**

f. Explain the sign at D. **slur, play the notes smoothly connected**

h. Define *andante*. **moderate walking pace**

i. Does this piece end on a stable or unstable scale degree? **stable**

j. Name the triad formed by the notes at E: **G major**

k. In this key, this triad is the: ❏ tonic triad    ☑ subdominant triad    ❏ dominant triad

Page 232

1. Who composed the music shown above? **George Frideric Handel**

2. What is the name of the composition? **Messiah - Hallelujah Chorus**

3. What key is it in? **D major**

4. What four voices are used to sing this piece? **soprano alto tenor bass**

5. Name the triad formed by the notes at A **D major triad**

6. Name the interval at B. **per 4**

7. Name the interval at C. **maj 3**

8. Name the interval at D. **per 5**

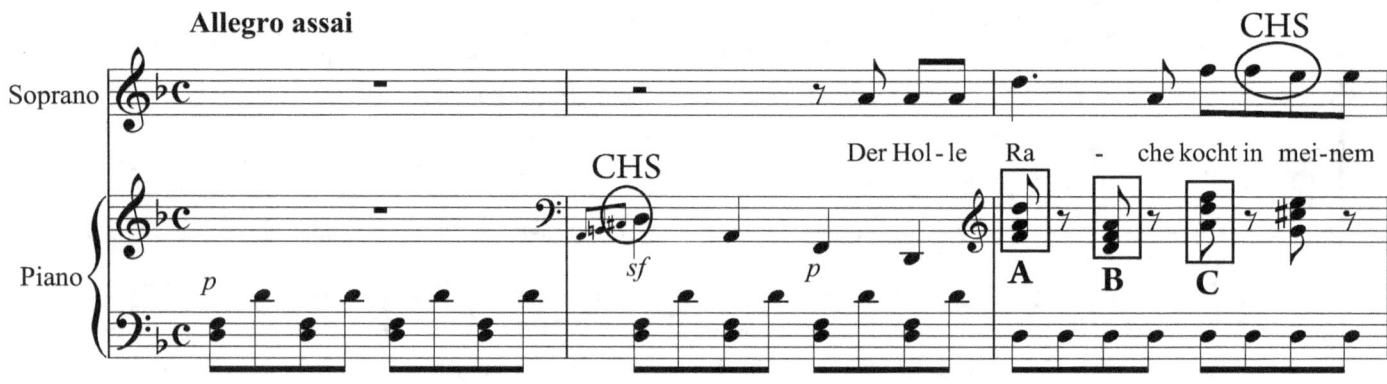

1. Who wrote the above musical example? **Wofgang Amadeus Mozart**

2. What musical era was it written? **Classical**

3. What character is singing in this passage? **The Queen of the Night**

4. In what language is she singing? **German**

5. What is the key of this piece? **D minor**

6. Name the triad and inversion at A: **D minor 1st inversion**
   B: **D minor Root position**
   C: **D minor 2nd inversion**

7. Circle one chromatic half step on the score. Label it CHS.

8. Define Allegro assai: **Very fast**

9. How many measures are in this example? **6**

# Sonatina

Cornelius Gurlitt
1820 -1901

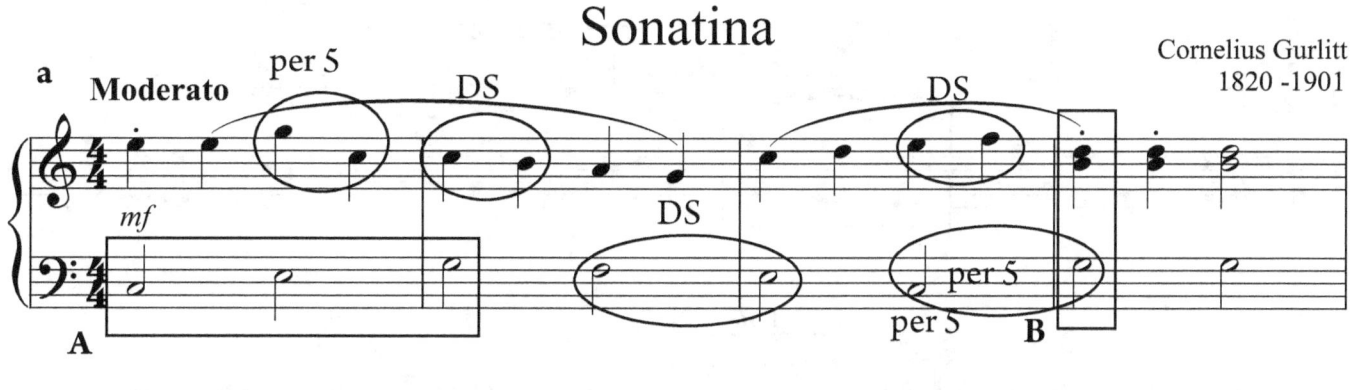

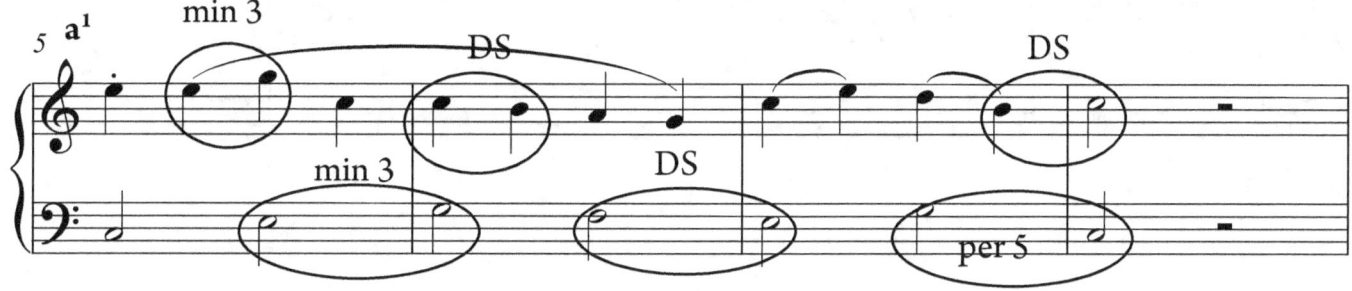

1. Name the composer of this piece? **Cornelius Gurlitt**

2. Name the key of this piece. **C major**

3. Write the time signature on the score.

4. Define "moderato" **at a moderate tempo or speed**

5. How many phrases are in this example? **2**

6. Does the first phrase end on a stable or unstable degree? **unstable**

7. Does the second phrase end on a stable or unstable degree? **stable**

8. Label the phrases either: (a - a¹⁾) or (a - b) depending on the form.

9. What triad is formed by the notes in the box at letter A: **C major triad**

10. What triad is formed by the notes in the box at letter B: **G major triad**

11. Find the interval of a harmonic minor 3rd, circle it, and label it maj 3.

12. Find the interval of a melodic perfect 5th, circle it, and label it per 5.

13. Find two different diatonic semitones, circle them, and label them DS.

14. How many slurs occur in this piece? **5**

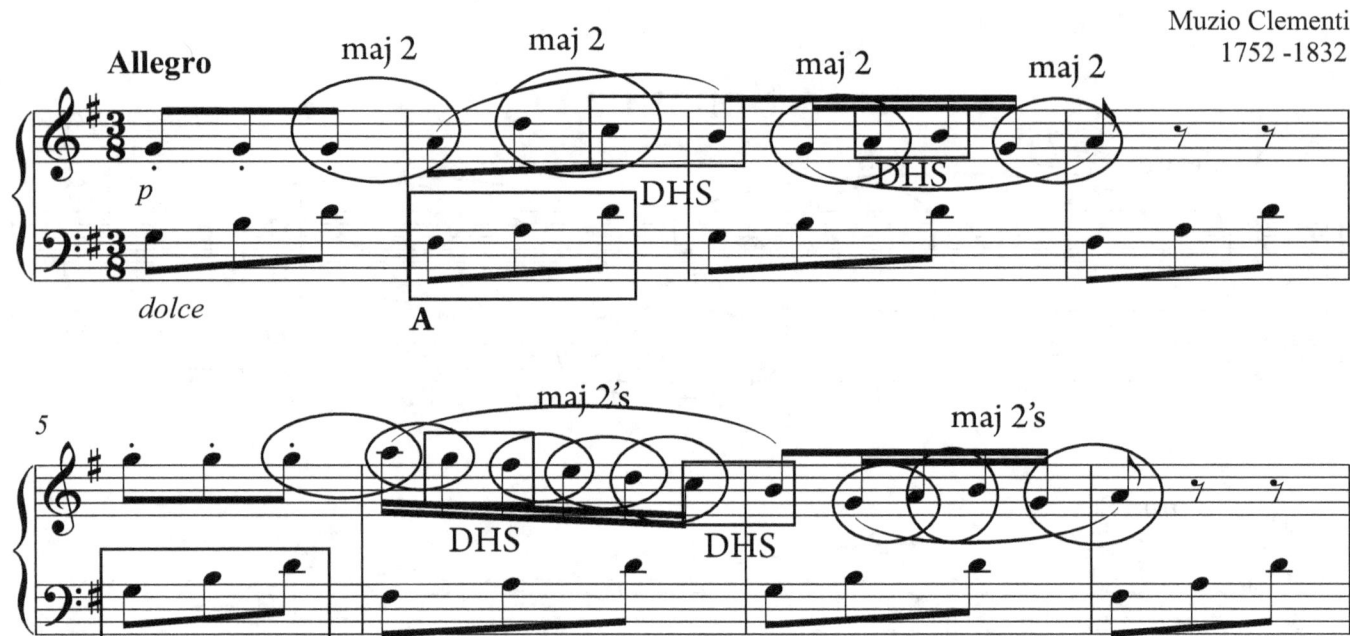

1. Name the composer of this piece? **Muzio Clementi**

2. When did he live? **1752-1832**

3. Write the time signature on the score.

4. Name the key of this piece. **G major**

5. Define "allegro." **fast**

6. Define "dolce." **sweetly**

7. For the triad at letter A, name the: Root **D**   Quality **major**   Position **1st**

8. For the triad at letter B, name the: Root **G**   Quality **major**   Position **root**

9. How many times does the broken tonic triad occur in the bass clef. **4**

10. Find a melodic major 2nd, circle it and label it maj 2.

11. Find a melodic major 3rd, circle it and label it maj 3.

12. Find a diatonic half step, put a box around it and label is DHS.

1. Name the key of this piece? **F major**

2. Write the time signature on the score.

3. Check the terms that apply to this time signature.  ☑compound   ☐triple   ☐simple   ☑duple

4. Mark the phrases with a slur.

5. Label each phrase using the letters *a, a¹* or *b*.

6. Define "andantino." **a little faster than andante**

7. Name the triad at letter A.   root: **F**   quality: **major**

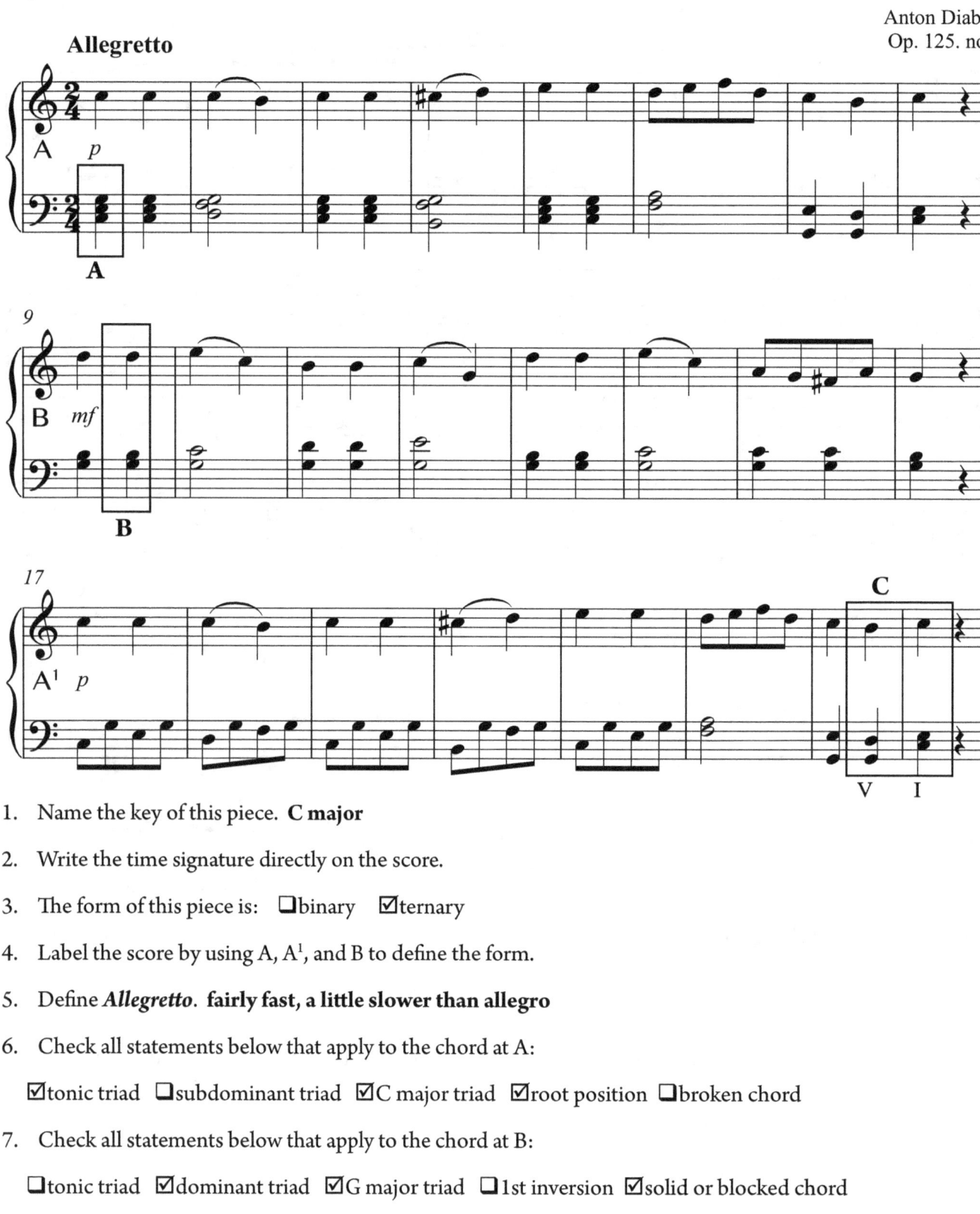

1. Name the key of this piece. **C major**
2. Write the time signature directly on the score.
3. The form of this piece is:  ☐binary   ☑ternary
4. Label the score by using A, A¹, and B to define the form.
5. Define *Allegretto*. **fairly fast, a little slower than allegro**
6. Check all statements below that apply to the chord at A:

   ☑tonic triad  ☐subdominant triad  ☑C major triad  ☑root position  ☐broken chord

7. Check all statements below that apply to the chord at B:

   ☐tonic triad  ☑dominant triad  ☑G major triad  ☐1st inversion  ☑solid or blocked chord

8. Name the cadence at C:

   ☑perfect authentic cadence   ☐half cadence   ☐imperfect authentic cadence

9. Symbolize the chords of this cadence on the score using functional chord symbols.

Page 242

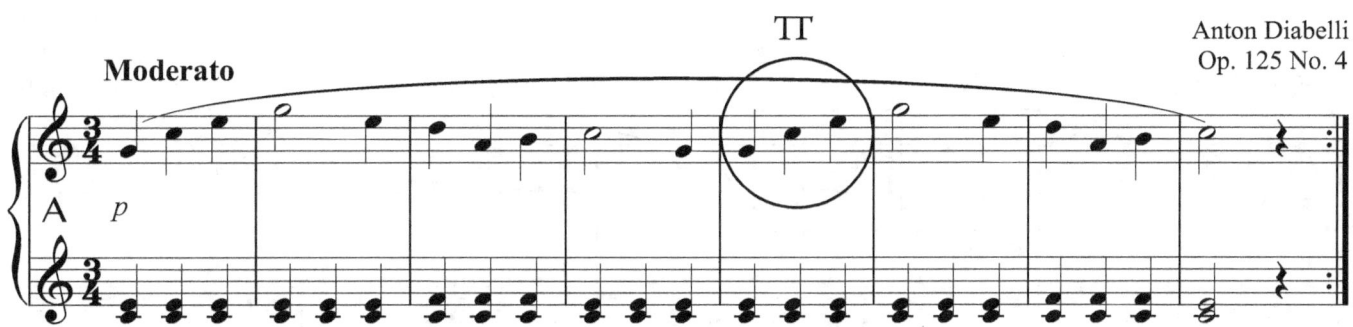

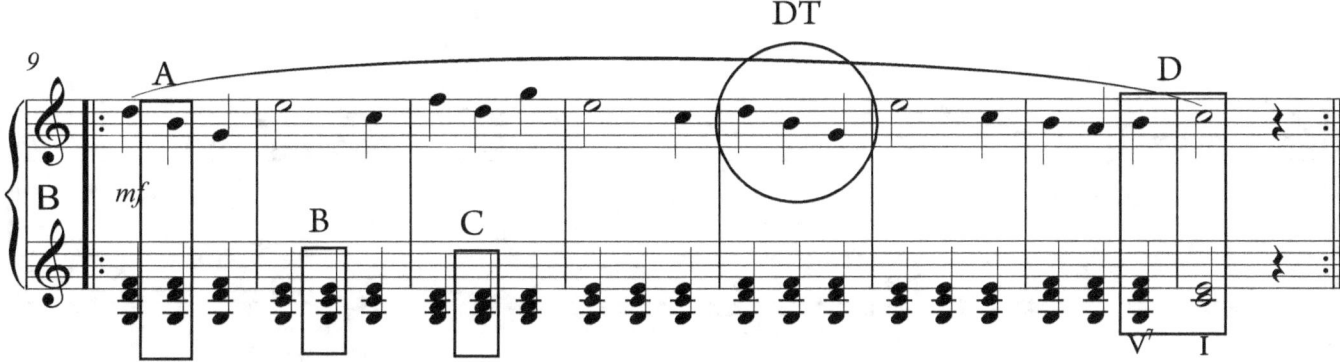

1. Name the key of this piece. **C major**

2. Write the time signature directly on the score.

3. Check the words below that apply to this time signature.

    ☑triple   ☐compound   ☐duple   ☑simple   ☐quadruple

4. Mark the phrases using a slur.

5. The form of this piece is:   ☑binary   ☐ternary

6. Label the score by using A, A¹, and B to define the form.

7. Define *Moderato*. **at a moderate speed or tempo**

8. Name the chord at letter A: **G⁷, the dominant 7th**

9. For the chord at letter B name the: root **C**   quality **major**   position **2nd inv.**

10. For the chord at letter C name the: root **G**   quality **major**   position **root pos.**

11. The cadence at D is:   ☐half   ☑perfect authentic   ☐imperfect authentic

12. Write the functional chord symbols for this cadence directly on the score.

13. Find and circle a broken dominant triad on the score. Label it DT.

14. Find and circle a broken tonic triad on the score. Label it TT.

Page 243

Joseph Haydn
(1732-1809)
Sonata Hob XVI 34, III

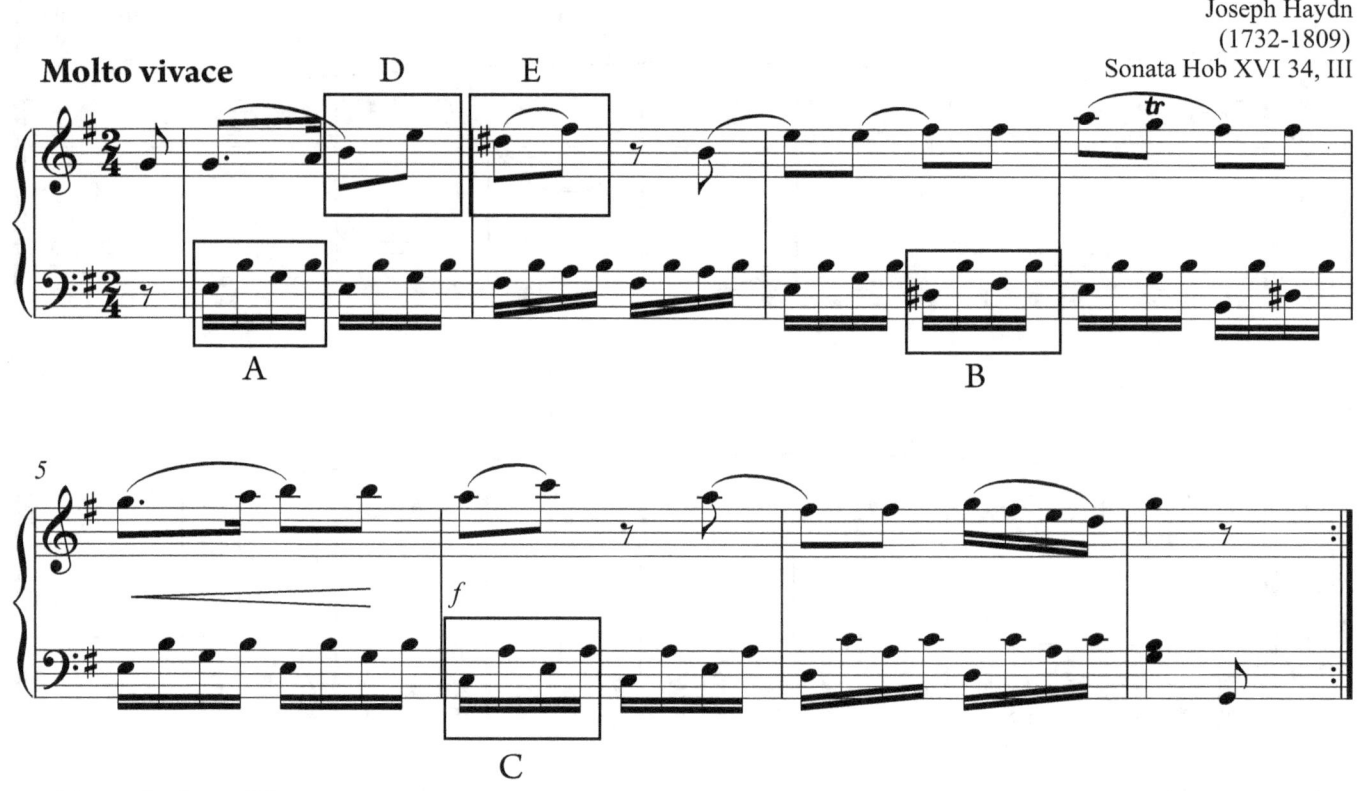

1. Name the key of this piece. **E minor**

2. Write the time signature directly on the score.

3. This excerpt is written for a right hand melody with left hand accompaniment. This is and example of:

    ❑polyphonic music   ☑homophonic music   ❑contrapuntal music   ❑absolute music

4. What musical era was this piece composed? **Classical**

5. Name the chord at A:   root **E**   quality **minor**   position **root pos**

6. Name the chord at B:   root **B**   quality **major**   position **1st inv**

7. Name the chord at C:   root **A**   quality **minor**   position **1st inv.**

8. In this piece, chord A is the:   ☑tonic triad   ❑subdominant triad   ❑dominant triad

9. In this piece, chord B is the:   ❑tonic triad   ❑subdominant triad   ☑dominant triad

10. In this piece, chord C is the:   ❑tonic triad   ☑subdominant triad   ❑dominant triad

11. Define *Molto vivace*: **Very lively**

12. This excerpt is an example of a:   ❑parallel period   ☑contrasting period

13. Name the interval at D: **min 3**

14. Name the interval at E: **per 4**

Page 249, No. 1  **Level 5 Exam**

B  A  G#  D  A

Page 249, No. 2

DHS  WS  CHS  DHS  DHS

Page 249, No. 3

Page 250, No. 4

maj 3         maj 7         per 5         min 6         maj 2

Page 250, No. 5

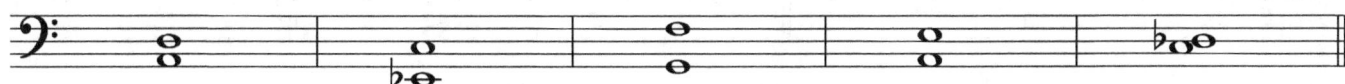

Page 250, No. 6

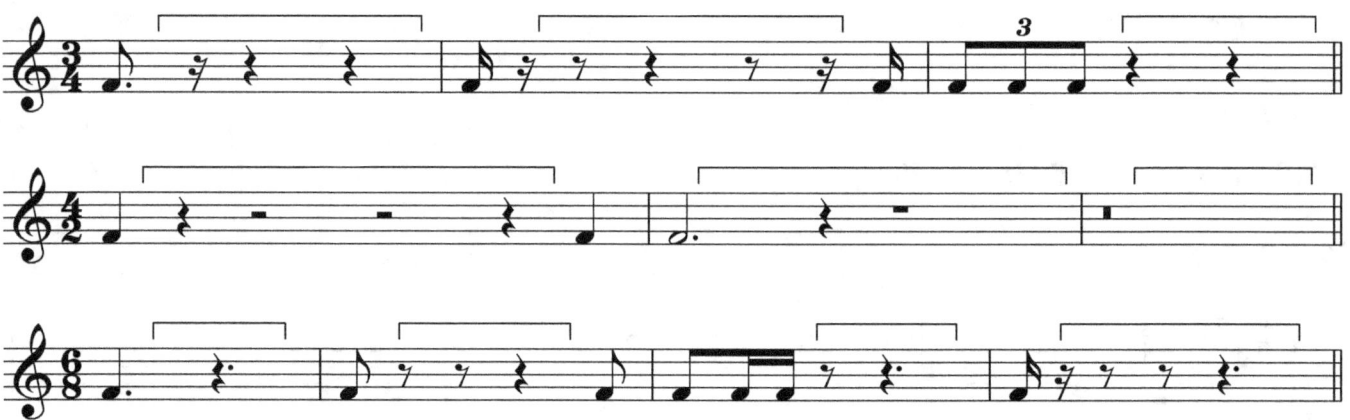

Page 250, No. 7

W.A. Mozart
Concerto K218

D major

Page 251, No. 8

F major

Page 251, No. 9

i.　　　　　ii.　　　　　iii.　　　　　iv.　　　　　v.

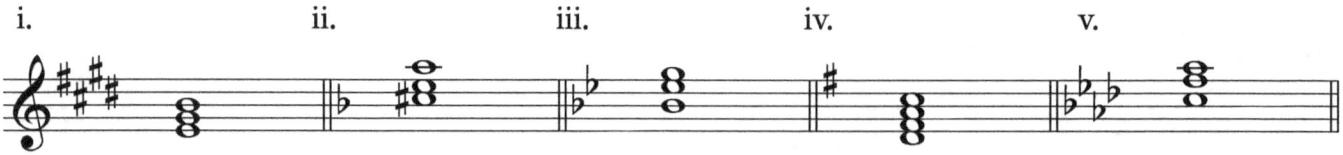

Page 251, No. 10

i)
h)
e)
f)
j)
a)
g)
d)
b)
c)

Page 252, No. 11

andantino - a little faster than andante

larghetto - fairly slow, not as slow as largo

rubato - flexible tempo with slight variations of speed to enhance musical expression

largo - very slow

mano destra - right hand

poco - little

lento - slow

pedale - pedal

spiritoso - spirited

marcato - well marked or stressed

prestissimo - as fast as possible

tranquillo - tranquil

dolce - sweetly

leggiero - light

molto - much, very

espressivo - expressive

vivace - lively

fine - the end

marcato - well marked

adagio - slow

Page 253, No. 12

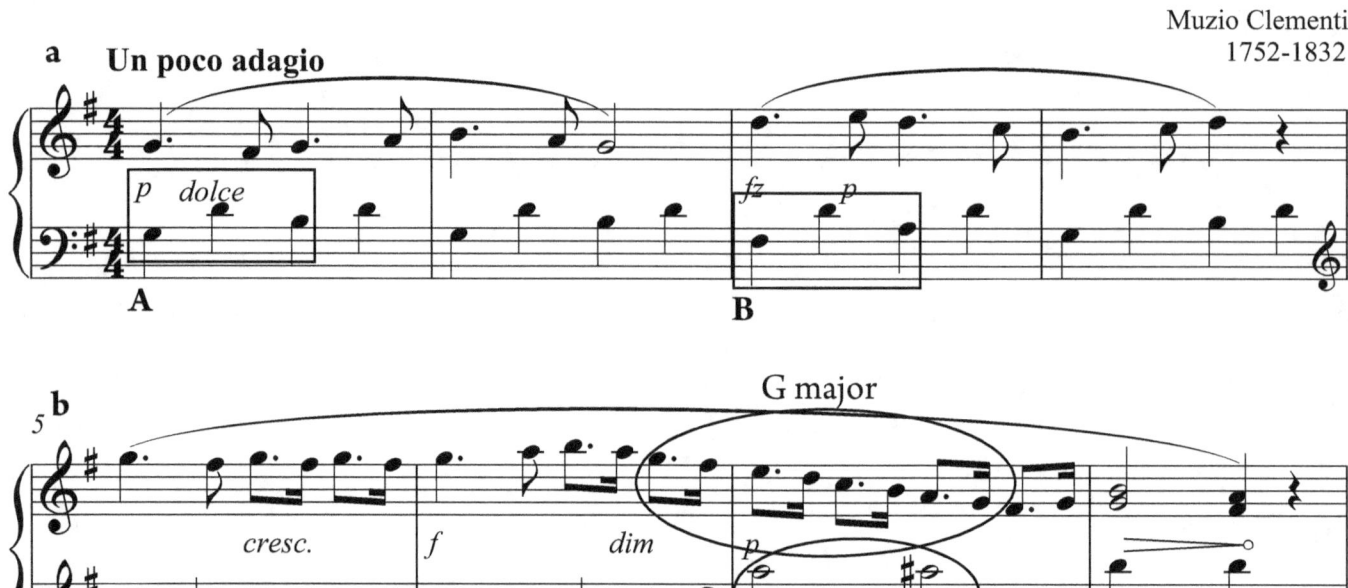

Muzio Clementi
1752-1832

1. What is the key of this piece? **G major**

2. Write the time signature on the score.

3. Define *dolce*     **sweetly**

4. Define *Un poco adagio*     **a little slow**

5. Label the two phrases as: a - a¹ or a - b.

6. For the triad at A, name the: Root: **G**   Quality: **major**   Position: **root**

7. For the triad at B, name the: Root: **D**   Quality: **major**   Position: **1st inversion**

8. Find a chromatic half step in the score. Circle it and label it: CHS.

9. Find and circle a G major scale on the score. Label it: G major.

10. Name the highest note in this piece.   **B**

Page 254, No. 1  **Level 6 Exam**

dim 5    dim 3    min 6    dim 8    maj 2

Page 254, No. 2

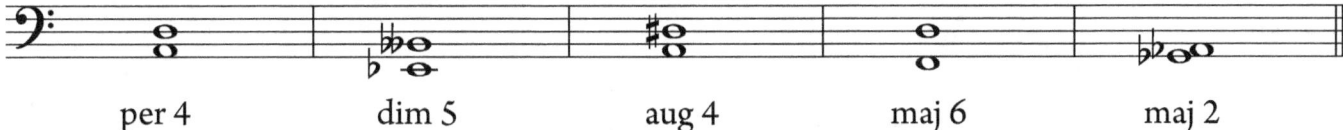

Page 254, No. 3

Page 254, No. 4

Page 255, No. 5

Page 255, No. 6

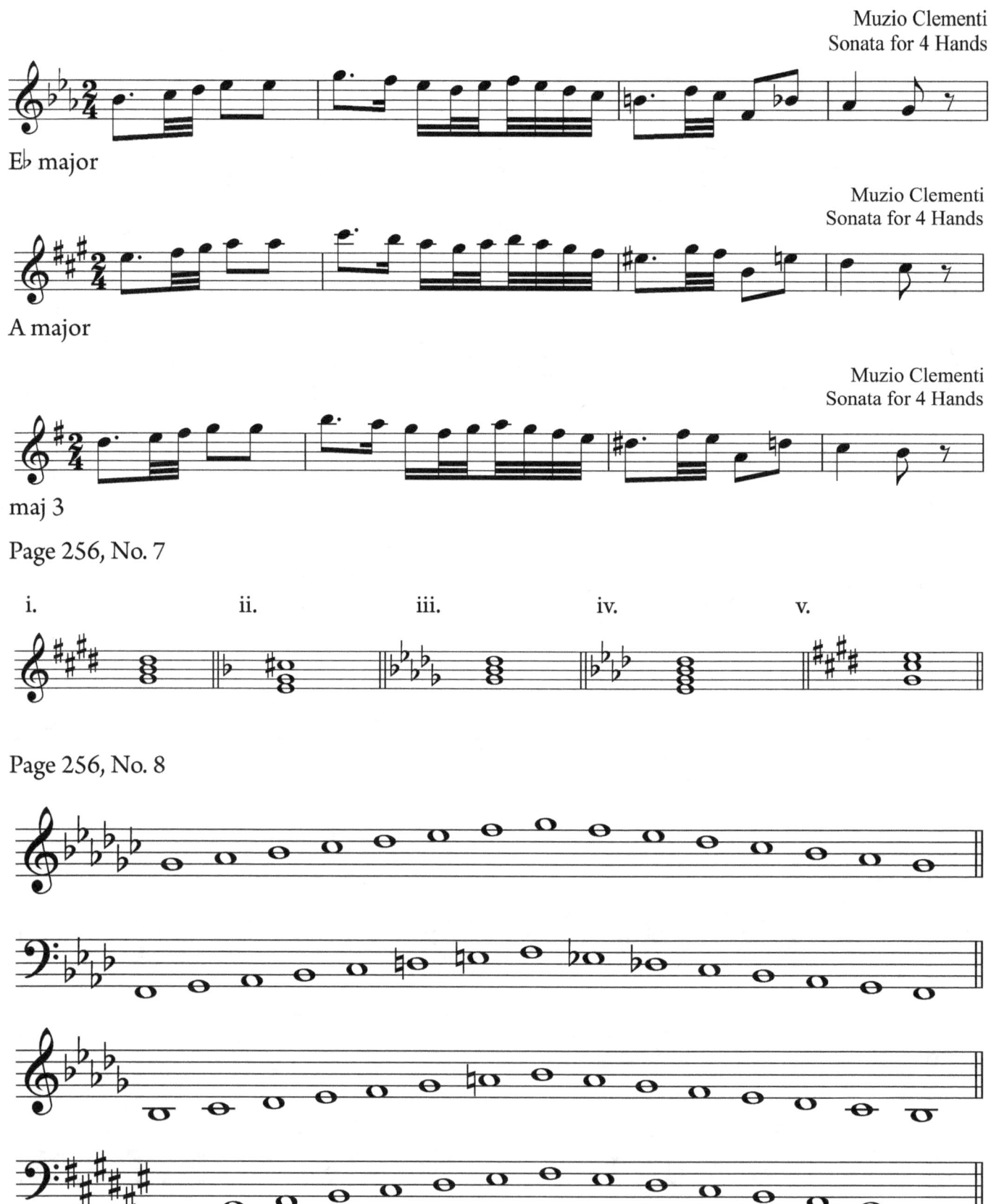

E♭ major

A major

maj 3

Page 256, No. 7

Page 256, No. 8

Page 257, No. 9

B♭ major

        B♭    F
        I     V
        half

        F    B♭
        V    I
        perfect authentic

Page 257, No. 10

h  g  d  i  f  c  e  b  a

Page 257, No. 11

**a. *animato***    lively, animated
**b. *con fuoco***    with fire
**c. *piu mosso***    more motion, movement
**d. *senza***    without
**e. *subito***    suddenly

Page 258 No. 12

1. What is the key of this piece? **G major**
2. Write the time signature on the score.
3. In what era was this composed? **classical**
4. Define *Allegretto espressivo* **fairly fast and expressive**
5. For the triad at A, name the: Root: **G**  Quality: **major**  Inversion: **root pos**
6. For the triad at B, name the: Root: **E**  Quality: **minor**  Inversion: **root pos**
7. Find a diatonic half step in the score. Circle it and label it: DHS.
8. Find a broken C major triad on the score. Circle it and label it: C major.
9. Name the interval at C. **aug 4**

www.ingramcontent.com/pod-product-compliance
Lightning Source LLC
Chambersburg PA
CBHW081729100526
44591CB00016B/2554